In the
PROVIDENCE
Of GOD

In the
PROVIDENCE
Of GOD

"You gave me life
and showed me kindness,
and in your providence
watched over my spirit"
(Job 10:12 NIV).

GOD'S PRESERVATION AND PROTECTION OF
George Neuvirth

PART 1: IN THE PROVIDENCE OF GOD
By: George Neuvirth
Copyright © 2009
GOSPEL FOLIO PRESS
All Rights Reserved

Published by
GOSPEL FOLIO PRESS
304 Killaly St. W.
Port Colborne, ON L3K 6A6
CANADA

Paper ISBN: 9781926765013
Hard Cover ISBN: 9781926765051
Cover design by Rachel Brooks
Author photo on Cover: © Vic Moss/Moss Photography

All photos, unless otherwise noted,
are the property of the Neuvirth family

PART 2: OUT OF HUNGARY ESCAPING THE
NAZI HOLOCAUST SOVIET COMMUNISM
Previously Published by © 2000, George Neuvirth
Armadillo Publishing Corporation, Georgetown, Texas 78627-2052

Printed in USA

Contents

PART 1
IN THE PROVIDENCE OF GOD

PART 2
Out of Hungary
Escaping Nazi Holocust & Soviet Communism
A True Story About Political Horror and Faith

CONTENTS

* Chapter 35 (Gen. 1:1), Chapter 36 (Matt. 16:3), Chapter 37
(Matt. 24:7), Chapter 38 (Matt. 12:25), Chapter 39 (Rom. 13:1),
Chapter 40 (1 Thess. 5:2), Chapter 41 (Matt. 7:15), Chapter
42 (John 8:32), Chapter 43 (Matt. 10:14), Chapter 44 (Ex. 3:8)

I would like to thank Anne Swartley and John Ohlmann for their help in putting this volume together. They are my dear friends with whom I truly enjoy times of fellowship centered on God's eternal word.

I would like to thank Gospel Folio Press for their efforts in bringing this book to publication. They are truly an answer to an old man's prayers. God bless them. My hope and prayer is that those who read this book would be encouraged to trust in God and be built up in their faith.

—George Neuvirth

Foreword

"You gave me life and showed me kindness,
and in Your providence watched over my spirit"
(Job 10:12, NIV).

God is at work in each of our lives, in all of our circumstances. We may be completely unaware of His handiwork unless we look back on the events of our lives in the light of God's Word. This book is the testimony of such a man, a faithful servant who has been careful to give thanks.

George Neuvirth has lived through some extraordinary experiences, situations most of us can hardly imagine. He was born in 1926, into a prominent Hungarian–Austrian family in Budapest. As a teenager he survived the Nazi occupation in World War II, and the Siege of Budapest (1944–45). He then had to endure the repressive Communist regime in Hungary under which his family lost everything. At the age of twenty, God drew George to Himself by grace, through faith in Jesus Christ. This took place through the circumstance of the death of his mother in 1946. After his father died in 1952, and the 1956 Hungarian uprising failed, George became a refugee, and came to America. Here he became a teacher of history and foreign languages. He married Jane Rawlings in 1961. They moved to Colorado, had two children, and enjoyed many years of ministry together.

As George Neuvirth has examined his life in terms of God's purpose—that of glorifying Himself through His servant George—so may we examine our lives, and understand and praise the Lord, Jesus Christ, for His work in us.

Space is given for recording your thoughts on how the Lord has provided for you.

John Ohlmann
Highlands Ranch, Colorado
August 2009

IMÁDOTT
ÉDES ANYÁMNAK

özv. NEUVIRTH NÁNDORNÉ
MUNKÁCSI
SÜTŐ AMÁLIA
MEGHALT 1930 FEBRUÁR 5.
Dr. NEUVIRTH ALFRÉDNÉ
NEUWALDER PAULA
1946 x.1.
Dr. NEUVIRTH ALFRÉD
1952 ÁPRILIS. 27.

IN MEMORY OF MY PARENTS
Dr. Alfred and Mrs. Paula Neuvirth

The memory of my parents is very dear to me. Ensuring that they are not forgotten gives me great satisfaction, and it is in their memory that I have written these few pages.

My father loved his mother dearly, and he often reminded me that the love parents have for their child is a great blessing in that child's life. My parents did love and care for me, especially through great dangers and deprivation.

Sadly, my parents could not accompany me very far along my life's journey. They both died too early, and in miserable circumstances in Hungary after World War II. They were not able to see how God continued to protect me, and lead me step by step.

In Budapest, there is nothing left of our family but a grave where my grandmother lies, along with my father and mother. On the marble stone that marks it the epitaph is illustrated by a carving of a young man burying his head in his mother's shoulder, mourning.

George Neuvirth
Littleton, Colorado
August 2009

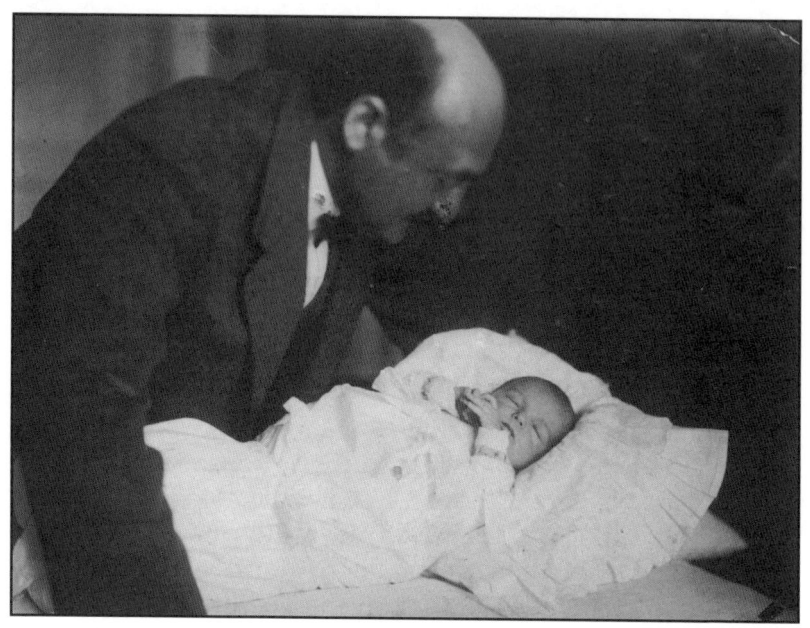

Dr. Alfred Neuvirth with his son George

Mrs. Paula Neuvirth and young George

1

You knitted me together in my mother's womb

My father was Hungarian. His father was of German descent, from Saxony, and his mother from an old Hungarian family. My mother was Viennese. Her parents were Jewish merchants who had a leather goods store on Der Graben, the Fifth Avenue of Vienna, in Austria.

My parents met when my father was on a trip to Vienna. After they were married they moved to Budapest. My parents were over forty, and I was to be their first, and, as it turned out, only child. In 1925—though I was expected with joy—such a pregnancy for parents of their age was dangerous, even life-threatening for the mother. One of my treasured possessions is a letter my father wrote to my mother while he was away on business when she was pregnant. He urged her to take care of herself and rest. I was born safely in January 1926. I praise God that my parents received me with so great a love and were so careful to provide me with a loving, caring home during the difficult times that were to follow.

"For You formed my inward parts; You knitted me together in my mother's womb. I praise You, for I am fearfully and wonderfully made. Wonderful are Your works; my soul knows it very well. My frame was not hidden from You, when I was being made in secret, intricately woven in the depths of the earth. Your eyes saw my unformed substance; in Your book were written, every one of them—the days that were formed for me—when as yet there were none of them" (Ps. 139:13–16).

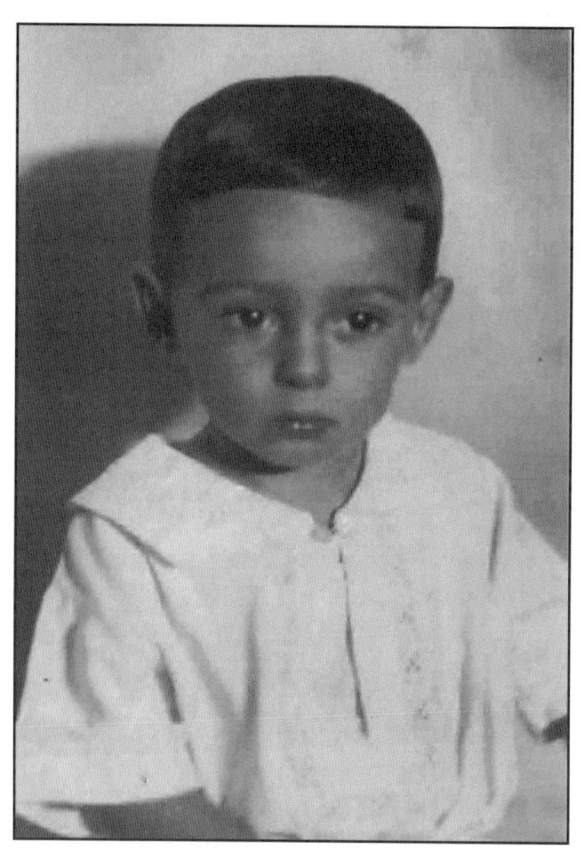

George (circa 1930)

2

Bless the LORD . . .
who heals all your diseases

At the age of four, I fell and injured myself. The wound developed an infection that spread throughout my body. I became very listless, and no one knew what was wrong. Our doctor said only one hope remained; perhaps a famous Viennese surgeon—who was arriving by train that same evening—might have the answer. At that time, Vienna was a center for medical study and training. The next day this surgeon examined me and pointed to my side: "Here is the abscess. Here we need to cut." The operation saved my life. One more day without that surgery and I would have died.

"Bless the LORD, O my soul, and all that is within me, bless His holy name! Bless the LORD, O my soul, and forget not all His benefits, Who forgives all your iniquity, Who heals all your diseases, Who redeems your life from the pit, Who crowns you with steadfast love and mercy, Who satisfies you with good so that your youth is renewed like the eagle's" (Ps. 103:1–5).

George and Mrs Paula Neuvirth

3

The LORD set His heart in love on your fathers

When I was fifteen my mother asked me if I would mind being Jewish. I said that I would mind, that I didn't want to be Jewish. This was the prevailing sentiment in most of Europe at that time. I did not realize how important that question would become. Nor did I understand that I was breaking my mother's heart.

The fact that my mother was Jewish was not a problem until Hungary allied itself with Nazi Germany in 1938. In Germany, the Nuremberg Laws did not allow a citizen to have any Jewish blood, back through both sets of grandparents, but in Hungary regulations were not so strict initially. In September 1939, we had to take our family papers to a military office for identification. The officer who reviewed them said my father's "Aryan blood saved your son from being a Jew."

After the war I learned what it means to truly become one of God's chosen ones, part of the true Israel. It required the conversion of my heart through faith in Jesus Christ. I would answer my mother's question so differently now! I would run to her, embrace her, and tell her how much I love her and how blessed I am to be Jewish, and to have been found and forgiven by the Jewish Messiah.

"Yet the LORD set his heart in love on your fathers and chose their offspring after them, you above all peoples, as you are this day . . . For the LORD your God is God of gods and Lord of lords" (Deut. 10:15, 17a).

The Danube River flowing through Budapest

4

You . . . lay Your hand upon me

In early 1944 the Germans needed to build airstrips in the eastern part of Hungary, and they used high school students to do this. My gym teacher chose a number of us to go to Karcag for this work. An internment camp for Jews was near our worksite, and once another student told me that someone in that camp told him that I looked Jewish. I could have easily ended up in a death camp. Many people who were part Jewish did.

"O Lord, You have searched me and known me! You know when I sit down and when I rise up; You discern my thoughts from afar. You search out my path and my lying down and are acquainted with all my ways. Even before a word is on my tongue, behold, O Lord, You know it altogether. You hem me in, behind and before, and lay Your hand upon me. Such knowledge is too wonderful for me; it is high; I cannot attain it" (Ps. 139:1–6).

Bridge over the Danube River

5

If you lie down, you will not be afraid

In September 1944, while I was still in eastern Hungary, the Russian Army broke through the passes of the Carpathian Mountains, about two hundred miles to the east. All of us students were suddenly on our own to get home the best way we could. I chose to go home (to the west) by going east, to the town of Debrecen, the center of Hungarian Protestantism, and even closer to the advancing Red Army. I wanted to see a famous reformed theological seminary there.

Late in the evening, tired and cold, I went to the seminary and asked if I could spend the night. I was put in a room with two other students, and fell asleep as they talked with each other. In the morning they told me I had slept through a long air raid and bombing attack! The war was coming closer.

My decision to go to Debrecen was very foolish, and put me in great danger. The Allied bombing might have leveled the building where I slept. Or the Russian Army could have overrun the city—this happened a few weeks later—and I might have been killed, or captured and sent to a Soviet labor camp. This happened to the son of my parents' friends, and we heard that it happened to many others.

"My son, do not lose sight of these—keep sound wisdom and discretion, and they will be life for your soul and adornment for your neck. Then you will walk on your way securely, and your foot will not stumble. If you lie down, you will not be afraid; when you lie down, your sleep will be sweet" (Prov. 3:21–24).

Neuvirth Home
Where George was Born.

6

The LORD will keep your going out and your coming in

Only a few days after I came home from Karcag and Debrecen an order came for the conscription of my class into the Hungarian army. Understandably, my mother was very upset. She packed my bag, and I walked to the city hall, where a long line of young men had already formed. We were to be shipped out within the hour to the Western Front to fight the Americans.

Suddenly my father appeared, saying to me, "Son, you will not go." He had always commanded the respect of the city's authorities. He entered the office of the military doctor and emerged a few minutes later with a paper excusing me from the army. I never was told what he said to the doctor, or what was written on the paper.

"The LORD will keep your going out and your coming in from this time forth and forevermore" (Ps. 121:8).

Victims of the Arrow Cross Party murder squads at the Maros Street
Jewish Hospital in Budapest, 1945*

7

In the day of trouble
the LORD delivers him

In October 1944, the Green Shirts of the Arrow Cross, Hungary's version of the Nazi SS, took over our country. (The Arrow Cross murdered ten to fifteen thousand Jews outright, and deported eighty thousand to their deaths in German concentration camps.) Within two weeks they were in our house.

It was afternoon, and I was taking a piano lesson while my father took his customary nap. Suddenly some Green Shirts forced their way into our house, demanding that I wake my father. We were herded into the living room, and ordered to sit quietly without moving. One aimed his gun at us, boasting that he had just killed seven Jews. My piano teacher was quite upset, and they eventually let her leave. They searched our house, claiming they were looking for Communist literature. They found none, but kept on digging through all of our possessions. Though they identified my mother as Jewish, and me as half Jewish, they did not harm us.

"In the day of trouble the LORD delivers him; the LORD protects him and keeps him alive" (Ps. 41:1b–2a).

8

How precious is
Your steadfast love, O God!

After the Arrow Cross troops finished their search of our house they took us to their headquarters for more questioning. We were held in a large room on the top floor of the building. Suddenly the air raid sirens sounded, and we were left there on the top floor while everyone else hurried to the shelters in the basement. Later someone came back for us, and took us down to safety in the basement. And when my mother began shivering because of the cold she was even given a blanket. We spent the night there, in the cold basement of the Arrow Cross headquarters.

"How precious is Your steadfast love, O God! The children of mankind take refuge in the shadow of Your wings" (Ps. 36:7).

9

You preserve my life

The next day our family was moved to a hotel that had been turned into a holding place for political prisoners. My mother was taken from us, as they kept the men and women separate. My father and I were crowded into a room with scores of other men, including a number with high-ranking social status—professors, parliamentarians, even a general. Many were taken out for interrogation, and often returned severely beaten.

Then my father and I were led together into a room with only one interrogator. He was polite, and did not harm us in any way. A few days later our names were called, we were told that we could leave, and we were reunited with my mother.

"Though I walk in the midst of trouble, You preserve my life" (Ps. 138:7a).

Soviet tanks and infantry pressing on the Germans
near Budapest 1944*

10

The LORD . . . has . . . shown His steadfast love to me when I was in a besieged city

As a young man of eighteen, I remember the nearly indescribable feeling of being a civilian in a city under siege, knowing that my life, as well as the lives of my loved ones, were at stake. The front line between the German and Russian forces reached the outskirts of Budapest in early November 1944, and on December 26, 1944, the Red Army completed their encirclement of our city. Escape was no longer possible. We lost our access to water and gas for heat. One hundred thousand German and Hungarian troops were trapped. Stalin, the Soviet dictator, gave the Red Army a free hand, and the battle for Budapest began. Before the city surrendered unconditionally on February 13, 1945, it would be nearly destroyed.

"Blessed be the LORD, for He has wondrously shown His steadfast love to me when I was in a besieged city" (Ps. 31:21).

Hungarian Parliament Building

11

The Lord . . . does not willingly . . . grieve the children of men

Early in the siege the family of one of my closest friends, Francis Halász, had relocated to the Pest side of the Danube River that bisected the city. They thought that they would be safer there, but that area was one of the first to fall to the Red Army. They took all of the civilians—some tens of thousands—and interred them in prisoner-of-war camps outside the city. Francis died from one of the many diseases that broke out in those camps. He was just eighteen years old. My dear friend had to perish, just thirty miles from his home, in a prisoner-of-war camp.

"For the Lord will not cast off forever, but, though He cause grief, He will have compassion according to the abundance of His steadfast love; for He does not willingly afflict or grieve the children of men" (Lam. 3:31–33).

German troops in Budapest, October 1944

12

He . . . remembered us in our low estate

During the siege our villa was occupied by the Germans, and we were moved down to the basement, which had a long, wide hallway with rooms on both sides. We slept in one dark, windowless room on beds made of planks spread across boxes, with mattresses on top.

A small iron stove burned a little coal, producing more smoke than heat. We were so cold that we had to wear our fur coats in the house. With the stove we were able to melt snow for drinking water and do some cooking. All we had to eat were beans and a little bread, and sometimes some meat from horses which had died on the roads nearby. It was so cold that the meat stayed fresh. We would carve chunks of meat from these carcasses, and cook them on our small stove.

"It is He who remembered us in our low estate, for His steadfast love endures forever; and rescued us from our foes, for His steadfast love endures forever; He who gives food to all flesh, for His steadfast love endures forever" (Ps. 136:23–25).

Highschool Plaque
"All Flesh is like grass."

13

All flesh is like grass

The Russians were shelling the city continually during the siege, and Allied bombers flew over every day. Our villa was hit several times, but the damage was not very great because the walls were two feet thick, and the roof was extraordinarily strong. One large bomb weighing fifty to one hundred pounds bored into the side of our house, but did not explode. A German soldier carried it out to the street on his shoulder!

We had flour for making bread, but not the means to bake it with our small stove, so I took the flour to the house of a family nearby who had a big oven. One day, when I went there, I found only half of a house. A shell had hit it, and the entire family was gone.

Sixty-four years later I went back to Budapest with my two children. I took them to my old high school where we saw several memorial plaques engraved with the names of teachers who had died in World War II. I remembered one of those teachers in particular because he had tutored me in math. The building where he lived was hit by a bomb, and his apartment was destroyed. He and his whole family were killed.

"All flesh is like grass and all its glory like the flower of grass. The grass withers, and the flower falls, but the word of the Lord remains forever" (1 Pet. 1:24–25a).

Neuvirth villa today

14

Through the valley of
the shadow of death

By late January 1945, all of the windows of our house had been blown out by the shockwaves from exploding bombs and shells. To keep out the worst of the cold we nailed plywood over the openings, leaving three-inch gaps at the top to let in some light. By now the fighting was all around us, as the armies were fighting street-to-street and house-to-house.

One day, as my father and I opened the door of one room and went in, a bullet came through the gap at the top of the window. It barely missed hitting me, boring into the wall before exploding. If I had been hit I probably would have been killed, because the Russians used "dum-dum" bullets that exploded on impact. A sharpshooter must have seen some light from the hallway through the gap at the top of the window.

"Even though I walk through the valley of the shadow of death, I will fear no evil, for You are with me; Your rod and Your staff, they comfort me" (Ps. 23:4).

Location where the Russian soldiers entered the Neuvirth villa

15

Do not be afraid of sudden terror

At the end of January 1945, there were about a dozen German soldiers stationed in our house. On February 1, their commander—a very brave man—told us to stay in the basement because the Russians were about to attack our house. Within minutes of his warning, a Russian grenade exploded in our boiler room, and the Russians entered our house through the basement. It was chaos! In the dark, smoke from the explosion and gunfire made visibility even worse. All I could see were the red flashes of the guns firing. Explosions and gunfire all around. Bullets flying everywhere. It was a miracle that no one was killed.

We started shouting, "Civilians! Civilians!" Out of the darkness and noise stepped a young Russian soldier, no older than myself. He could have killed us, but he stopped shooting. This seemed very strange, since at that time in Budapest a piece of bread was worth more than a human life. The Russians continued to pour through the breach they had made in our basement. They were all camouflaged in white. They lined us up, and herded us into the boiler room.

Two armies—German and Russian—fighting in our home, fighting from room to room! It was incredible. It was a nightmare.

*"Do not be afraid of sudden terror, or of the ruin of the
wicked when it comes"* (Prov. 3:25).

Neuvirth villa street number.

16

A good name is to be more desired than great wealth

In the first week of February 1945, the Red Army took over our entire neighborhood. An officer sent me, with our gardener, to a Russian command post to be registered for identification purposes. My dear mother was very upset, and started to cry. An older Russian soldier tried to reassure her, explaining that her son would come back. The two of us were taken to another villa, where they interviewed the gardener first. I heard him say that my family was very well thought of; that we did not side with the Germans; and that we did not support or cooperate with the Arrow Cross. His kind words were a tremendous help.

Many people gave each other up at that time for no apparent reason. If the gardener had testified against us we would have been taken to a camp, tortured, and probably sent to an internment camp. My aging parents would surely have died even sooner than they did. I later tried to find the gardener to thank him for his testimony, but was unable to. I fear I never did thank him.

"A good name is to be more desired than great wealth; favor is better than silver and gold" (Prov. 22:1, NASB).

17

Save me from blood thirsty men

Every night that February the Russians would wake us by shining flashlights in our faces, and make us go outside to work. It did not matter to them whether or not we got any sleep. In the middle of the night, in the snow, we would have to carry shells and move cannons.

One night three Russian soldiers appeared in our basement. They pointed to my parents and me, ordered us out into the yard, and said they were going to shoot us. We were filled with fear, but slowly followed them outside. We were sure we were minutes, if not seconds, from death. Suddenly a Russian officer appeared, and the soldiers—who were drunk—scattered.

"Deliver me from those who work evil, and save me from bloodthirsty men" (Ps. 59:2).

18

The LORD is your keeper

The Russian soldiers used civilians for dangerous jobs as our lives were of little value to them. One night in February 1945, they ordered my father to go down the road to find out just where the German lines were. As he was walking in the deep snow he encountered a German patrol. To immediately turn back would have looked suspicious, so he kept on walking. The German soldiers asked him where he was going. My father answered immediately that he was going to the drugstore, and kept on walking. Suddenly the soldiers began shouting that there was no drugstore around, and started shooting at him, but by then he was out of range and was not hit. He returned home by another way. Though I was unaware at that time that it was God who protected him, I was very thankful my father was spared that night.

"The LORD is your keeper; the LORD is your shade on your right hand. The sun shall not strike you by day, nor the moon by night. The LORD will keep you from all evil; He will keep your life" (Ps. 121:5–7).

Street scene after the Siege of Budapest1945

Taken in Budapest by a soviet photographer, March 1945. Source:
http://victory.rusarchives.ru/catalogue/ photo.php?photo_id=306&id=6

19

He . . . [made] my steps secure

Even before the battle for Budapest was over the Russians made us labor for them, digging trenches and building walls. The temperature was below zero, it was snowing, and the ground was frozen. It was very difficult work. We were warned to return home by a route different from the one we had taken to get to the work site, because other groups of Russian soldiers were rounding up civilians to put them in prisoner-of-war camps. Even though the Russians made me toil in these work parties many times, I always returned home safely.

I still am amazed that I was never taken to a Russian prison camp. So many of my friends, so many young people, were taken away to these camps. The son of some family friends who had been sent to Russia earlier was finally returning home, when he was picked up again on the outskirts of Budapest, and shipped off to a camp in Siberia for another five years. It is miraculous that I was kept safe and in the company of my family during those terrible times.

"He drew me up from the pit of destruction, out of the miry bog, and set my feet upon a rock, making my steps secure" (Ps. 40:2).

LIEZEN - MAYER Sandor
Gyor, 1839-Munchen, 1898
Alvo no, 1867
Sleeping Woman, 1867*

* Painting formerly belonging to the Neuvirth Family.
Now in a Budapest museum.

20

He may deliver their soul from death and keep them alive in famine

On May 7, 1945, peace came to Europe. I did not know what peace was. I had become so accustomed to the hardships of war, and times were still very difficult. Rationing of food and fuel continued. Fresh fruit was practically nonexistent, and meat was a luxury.

Inflation was rampant. People had to carry their money in suitcases. Currency that had some value in the morning was worthless by evening. My father owned many valuable paintings that he was forced to barter for much of what we needed.

Housing was also a huge problem. So many buildings had been destroyed that people were crowded into the ones that remained. We ended up living in two rooms of our own house since all the other rooms had been assigned to strangers by the government. We all shared the kitchen and bathroom. Though this was a big change from our life before the war, we had a place to stay, and food to eat.

"The LORD looks down from heaven; He sees all the children of man; from where He sits enthroned He looks out on all the inhabitants of the earth, He who fashions the hearts of them all and observes all their deeds . . . Behold, the eye of the LORD is on those who fear Him, on those who hope in His steadfast love, that He may deliver their soul from death and keep them alive in famine" (Ps. 33:13–15, 18–19).

Mrs. Paula Neuvirth

21

I bowed down in mourning

Dance fever had taken over Europe, and big band music was playing everywhere. The tunes of George Gershwin, Cole Porter, and Glenn Miller became my songs.

But the hardships of the war, especially the siege, had taken their toll. My mother had not been well for some time, and in 1946 her condition worsened. She was very weak, though she tried to hide it from us. At first I didn't notice. I was too busy enjoying myself in the relaxed post-war atmosphere of Budapest. Then my mother had to go to the hospital, a makeshift sanitarium run by Catholic nuns. She was running a very high fever and they gave her many doses of penicillin, but she did not improve. My father said to me, "Son, your mother is very, very sick."

I was very troubled. Even during the worst of the war I had never thought that my mother might die. I became very uneasy and restless as I considered all the times I had been disrespectful, how I had so often disobeyed her, even been harsh with her. One evening at the hospital I sat down at her bedside. She was turned away from me so that I would not see how sick she was. I gathered my courage and asked, "Mother, can you forgive me for all the times I was disrespectful to you?" She turned to me and replied, "Of course, a mother can forgive her son." That was the last time I saw my mother alive. She died during the night, on October 1, 1946.

"I went about as though I grieved for my friend or my brother; as one who laments his mother, I bowed down in mourning" (Ps. 35:14).

22

Cut to the heart

I thought then that my mother's forgiveness would bring me peace from my uneasiness and restlessness, but they only worsened. Though I did not yet realize it, I needed to seek forgiveness from God.

Then a former schoolmate visited me and told me about a summer camp where he had "met Christ." I had never heard that someone could "meet Christ." He invited me to a Bible study for young people. Though I had gone to church, I had never been to a Bible study, or even read the Bible, because it seemed incomprehensible to me.

This Bible study was part of Christian Endeavor, or CE. At the study I felt comfortable from the start, as everyone there was about my age. When they started praying, it seemed to me that their prayers were real, that they were offered to One they knew personally. I had often prayed before falling asleep, but I did not know Who I was praying to, or how to approach Him properly. It felt like my prayers bounced off the ceiling.

After that first Bible study I went home and started reading my Bible. Slowly the words began to have meaning. I felt that they were directed at me. I began to understand that God loved me, and wanted me to love Him in return. I began to see that His love for me was both personal and everlasting: *"I have loved thee with an everlasting love: therefore with lovingkindness have I drawn thee"* (Jer. 31:3, KJV).

One night I read John 6:37: *"All that the Father giveth me shall come to me; and him that cometh to me I will in no wise cast out"* (KJV). Suddenly it hit me: Did this mean that if I came to Jesus, He would not cast me out, even with all of my flaws and sins? I was broken, cut to the heart. I told God that I could not solve my problems by myself, and that I would give my life to Him.

Then I had the peace I had been seeking because I knew that my sins had been forgiven. Christ had died on the cross for me. His sacrifice in my place, His blood, had washed away my guilt forever. At that point my life began to change.

"Now when they heard this they were cut to the heart, and said . . . 'What shall we do?'" (Acts 2:37).

23

It is the purpose of the LORD that will stand

In 1951, the deportations began. The Communists brought young peasants from the countryside to educate them in the Communist cause. They were given the homes and apartments of the upper middle class families, who were then sent to live in the peasants' previous homes. The people from the city had no choice. Sometimes their "new homes" were shacks with mud floors and mice running everywhere.

For six weeks in Budapest, the bell would ring at six o'clock in the morning. If your name was on the list, you had twenty-four hours to leave your home and go to your designated area. I thank God that my father was never on the list.

"Many are the plans in the mind of . . . man, but it is the purpose of the LORD that will stand" (Prov. 19:21).

Dr. Alfred Neuvirth
George's Father

24

For You have been my refuge

Not long after the deportations started my father became ill. I cannot recall ever seeing my father ill before this. His breathing was labored, and he had difficulty sleeping at night. I began to understand that I might lose my father as I had already lost my mother. He went into the hospital a couple of times, and the last time they moved him into the intensive care unit. At six o'clock in the evening, on April 27, 1952, he died. I was with him, and the last words he heard from me were that God loved him. With his death a whole era of my life was gone. I had no more family. I was on my own.

"Hear my cry, O God, listen to my prayer; from the end of the earth I call to You when my heart is faint. Lead me to the rock that is higher than I, for You have been my refuge, a strong tower against the enemy. Let me dwell in Your tent forever! Let me take refuge under the shelter of Your wings!" (Ps. 61:1–4).

25

I have learned in whatever situation I am to be content

After the war I had pursued a university education, receiving my doctorate in Law and Political Science in 1952. I had hoped for a job in a bank, or with the government, but such positions were closed to me since I was a member of the former bourgeois.

So I worked for the railroad carrying track. Then I worked in factories. I was considered a good worker, but once I was fired merely because my supervisor had taken a dislike to me. By the grace of God the factory manager let me go with the bland explanation "discharged with consent." He could have turned me over to the secret police for questioning.

If my life was hard, my outlook was good, because of Christ. Looking to Him brought me joy and security.

"I have learned in whatever situation I am to be content.
I know how to be brought low, and I know how to abound.
In any and every circumstance, I have learned the secret of
facing plenty and hunger, abundance and need. I can do all
things through Him who strengthens me" (Phil. 4:11–13).

26

For I know the plans I have for you

In the summer of 1956 there were signs of civilian unrest in Hungary. Then on October 23 students and others took to the streets of Budapest. For ten days Hungary was a free nation. But on November 4, 1956, Russian tanks rolled into Budapest, just as they had in 1945. In the end five thousand were dead and many more had been shipped to labor camps in the Soviet Union.

At the end of November I decided to leave Hungary. I had no family, no possibility of any meaningful vocation, and I had to endure continuing persecution for my former status and for my faith. After much prayer, and having sought the advice of other believers, I asked a friend to leave with me.

Early on the morning of November 26, 1956 we left my house for the last time. Although I knew it was for the best, and that God was calling me elsewhere, I felt a deep loss. I felt I was being cut off from my roots.

"For I know the plans I have for you, declares the LORD, plans for welfare and not for evil, to give you a future and a hope" (Jer. 29:11).

George Neuvirth, circa 1956

27

Your word is a lamp to my feet

We had no real plans the morning we left. We walked to the railroad station past the Russian tanks. Miraculously we were able to purchase tickets on the only train still running toward the Austrian border.

As the train approached the border the conductor warned us to get off before it got to the station at Hegyeshalom because the Hungarian secret police were watching it very closely. We got off at the stop before and started walking. A truck was passing filled with others headed for the border, and we climbed on. The truck stopped at a farmhouse, and we were told that someone would guide us to the border after dark. By the grace of God we were taken through both Hungarian and Russian lines, and crossed into Austrian territory sometime after midnight on November 27, 1956.

We stopped to rest by a haystack which kept us somewhat dry as it was a rainy night. In the morning we heard some people approaching. They were speaking German, not Hungarian or Russian, so we stood up so they could see us. They welcomed us as if we were long-lost friends!

The journey from Budapest to the Austrian border that day was relatively short—only about a hundred miles—but it was a very long emotional journey. I was leaving behind all that I had been, and I had no idea what was ahead. My future was in God's hands, and He was only going to show me that future one step at a time. My choice was clear. I needed to trust Him.

"Your word is a lamp to my feet and a light to my path"
(Ps. 119:105).

28

Wait for the LORD!

In Austria I stayed briefly with an uncle in Vienna, my mother's brother. He was very kind to me, and I have always been thankful to him for opening his home to me. I wrote to my parents' close friends, the Danos, who were now living in America, in New York. They responded with a telegram saying they were expecting me "with open arms."

Soon I was moved to a refugee camp near Salzburg to be taught how to live in America. Now, when I hear news about refugee camps, I know what the inhabitants are experiencing. The camps have there own reality, not just different from the life the refugees left behind, but different from the outside world. Everything you own is on a shelf above your bed, and your bed is the center of your world—you not only sleep on it, you live on it.

In the refugee camp I was becoming anxious and impatient. It is my nature to want to have everything now, in the present, right away and not later. But God operates on His timetable, not ours.

Looking back, that time now seems quite strange to me. It seemed like I was in that camp for a very long time, but it was only two weeks before my name appeared on the list of those who were to fly to America.

"Wait for the LORD; be strong and let your heart take courage; wait for the LORD!" (Ps. 27:14).

Camp Kilmer, NJ U.S. Army Photo

29

He will make straight your paths

On March 2, 1957, I arrived in America. I was placed in Camp Kilmer in New Jersey with other refugees. It was a former World War II training camp for the United States Army that had been reopened to accommodate us. My parents' dear friend and my sponsor, Mr. Danos, arrived at the camp and welcomed me. He and his wife were great friends to me for many years, treating me as their own son.

After ten days at Camp Kilmer, I traveled to Wichita, Kansas, where the First Presbyterian Church was helping with the relocation of refugees. The church arranged for me to live with a fine American family—the Amstutz family—and helped me get my first job—folding envelopes at a printing company for one dollar an hour. And I was learning English.

"Trust in the Lord with all your heart, and do not lean on your own understanding. In all your ways acknowledge Him, and He will make straight your paths" (Prov. 3:5–6).

Jane Rawlings

30

[He] will receive a hundredfold

At that time I was going to meetings of the First Presbyterian Youth Group. It was there that I first met Jane Rawlings, in the Fall of 1957. She was a teacher at a local high school. She encouraged me to go to Wichita State University to earn a teaching certificate. While I was there I joined InterVarsity Christian Fellowship, as the Lord had given me a heart for evangelism.

When I came to this country I left everything behind, save what I could carry. My parents were dead. My home had been taken over by the government. The Communist government was even trying to destroy or rewrite as much of Hungarian history as it could, as well as making the worship of God as difficult as possible. But now the Lord was already giving me so much more than all I had lost. He provided for all my needs, and then bestowed even more blessings.

"And everyone who has left houses or brothers or sisters or father or mother or children or lands, for My name's sake, will receive a hundredfold and will inherit eternal life" (Matt. 19:29).

George and Jane's Wedding

31

He who finds a wife
. . . obtains favor from the LORD

On a beautiful summer day, in her home town of Marshall, Missouri, I asked Jane to marry me, adding this very important question, "Will you serve the Lord with me?" She said yes. We were married on June 17, 1961. There followed forty-six years of a rich and fruitful marriage. We made a great team.

Both Jane and I were teachers: she taught English Composition, and I taught foreign languages and Western Civilization. We raised two children, Paul and Grace, and the Lord protected them from many of the troubles of our society. They matured into fine Christian people, with families of their own. Jane and I were also a team in spreading the Kingdom of God. Jane led Child Evangelism classes, and I was involved with the Salvation Army in their outreach to jailed prisoners. We also served Christ in many other ways in our church and in our community. And to this day God still gives me the opportunity to proclaim the gospel at the Denver Rescue Mission.

On January 8, 2008, my Jane was called out of this present evil age to be with our dear Lord and Savior, Jesus Christ. I miss her so much now, but look forward to being with her again in heaven, as we both stand in the presence of our God and Lord, and sing everlasting praises to Him for all He has done and all that He is.

"He who finds a wife finds a good thing and obtains favor from the LORD" (Prov. 18:22).

Jane and George Neuvirth, circa 1989

32

Citizens of Heaven

Now, my prayer is that you who use this book will be encouraged to trust in God, and to join me in praising *"the God and Father of our Lord Jesus Christ, the Father of mercies and God of all comfort, who comforts us in all our afflictions, so that we may be able to comfort those who are in any affliction, with the comfort with which we ourselves are comforted by God"* (2 Cor. 1:3–4).

Today the noises of my tumultuous past are mere faint echoes. What stands out vividly for me is how my Lord was my Shepherd, giving me such wonderful parents and my precious wife, and allowing me long years to serve Him, almost fifty of them with Jane.

These days, though unable to drive because of macular degeneration, through the kindness of dear brothers and sisters in Christ, God is still able to use me in ministering to others, and to encourage and challenge them in the Word. And several times a year I can still travel from my home in Colorado, primarily to see my children and grandchildren in California. This fellowship comforts me as my years extend and my body fails.

Though I miss my dear Jane, I am thankful she is with the Lord. And, as for me, with Paul, *"I press on toward the goal for the prize of the upward call of God in Christ Jesus. . . . Our citizenship is heaven, and from it we await a Savior, the Lord Jesus Christ"* (Phil. 3:14).

"Our citizenship is in heaven, and from it we await a Savior, the Lord Jesus Christ" (Phil. 3:20).

George and Jane 1994

Afterword

The power at work within us

Along with my attempts herein to praise God for His provisions, I am confessing that I did not recognize most of them as such at the time. It may seem that God's greatest acts of providence are revealed when we are presented with our "days of trouble," our greatest trials. My prayer is that the Lord will open our eyes to see that He is at work in and through us every day, effecting more than we can imagine or plan. And for what grand purpose? For the encouragement of our brothers and sisters in God's family, and for the enticement of those not yet within this blessed household.

"Now to Him who is able to do far more abundantly than all that we ask or think, according to the power at work within us, to Him be glory in the church and in Christ Jesus throughout all generations, forever and ever. Amen" (Eph. 3:20–21).

"But thanks be to God, who in Christ always leads us in triumphal procession, and through us spreads the fragrance of the knowledge of him everywhere. For we are the aroma of Christ to God among those who are being saved and among those who are perishing, to one a fragrance from death to death, to the other a fragrance from life to life" (2 Cor. 2:14–16b).[1]

---

1 Should a more complete account of my story interest the reader, please see the following insert of the book, *Out Of Hungary: Escaping the Nazi Holocaust and Soviet Communism*, by George Neuvirth (Georgetown, Texas: Armadillo Publishing Corporation, 2000).

Part 2

OUT OF HUNGARY

Escaping Nazi Holocaust & Soviet Communism

A True Story About Political Horror and Faith

Contents of previously published book
giving additional detailed information
of this amazing story that needed to be told.

George Neuvirth

"I love history and was gripped with the history of Hungary, torn with its struggle first with the Nazi regime and then Russian Communism. Your account of the brave stand of Hungary in the war brought tears to my eyes."

—Dr. Charles A. Ver Straten
former Senior Pastor of Mission Hills Baptist
Church Littleton, Colorado

"This is a powerful book and one that I trust will have a good ministry."

—Dr. John D. Morris
President, Institute for Creation Research El
Cajon, California

"This is a book that opens up facts from the past and makes the peculiar Hungarian circumstances comprehensible. It leads the reader into a true testimony for Christ, as the author found Peace and a new life in Him. The book also gives comfort to those who struggle with difficulties."

—Andrew Fay
Restorations, Hungarian National Gallery
Lecturer, New York, Amsterdam

"Reading your book was a very special experience. Thank you for sharing your life story in a way that glorified our Lord. The history included was remarkable. "

—Marvin Anderson
Associate Professor, University of Colorado
Denver, Colorado

Preface

I am pushing the door open at the Adams County Detention Center in Brighton, Colorado. After being identified, I go down the steps where the inmates are. I see no bars, only open areas and "pods" with iron doors. I get a key and open the door of the big room, where the inmates come for my Bible study. As we sing, pray, and read the Word of God, I am aware that if not for the Grace of God, I would not be standing before them. I share this thought with the group. This awareness of my new life in Him, since I accepted Jesus Christ as my personal Saviour so many years ago, always keeps a song in my heart. Because I am so full of peace and thanksgiving, I want to share my story with you. . .

Imagine you're an upper-class male who summers in Switzerland and comes home to your parents' mansion overlooking Budapest, when it still claimed the title, "Paris of the East." It's 1939, and you're a young teenager, ready to begin high school. You have a good life before you. Then Hitler annexes Austria, of which Hungary shares a governing alliance. In the near future, your homeland must decide to take sides with either the Axis Powers or the Allies. It wants neither, but eventually makes a deal with Germany, opening its doors to Nazi terrorism and surrendering its Jews to certain death.

Your mother is Jewish, but your father's Aryan blood saves all of you. The Germans turn your home into a party headquarters, permitting you and your family to live in the basement. Once, you are interrogated and then jailed in a hotel room with twenty other men. Another time you are sent to work in a labor camp. You are then called to fight on the Western Front, but are spared from going.

As the end of the Second World War approaches, the Russians surround Budapest. The ensuing six-week siege debilitates the city's sources of water, food, and heat. Then the Russians break through and your street becomes a barb-wired war zone. Your backyard becomes a cemetery for German soldiers. You don't like the Germans, but you will like the Russians even less.

The best years of your life have been swallowed up by blackouts and air raids. You will not know physical freedom again until you escape Hungary after its short-lived revolution, a decade later. Your parents will have died and you will be sharing your house with "comrades," when you were once the only child of a wealthy merchant. You don't whine, however, because you have met someone who gives you hope, love, and peace in your heart. A National Revival has introduced you to Jesus Christ, your Personal Saviour. He is your friend, your comfort, your way to spiritual freedom.

Although you've been able to earn a Law degree, the Communist regime sentences you to a lifetime of mundane jobs, simply because you had been one of the bourgeois. By 1956, after the war, your city and your life have been ravaged by a Nazi dictatorship, a crippling siege, and Communist rule. You witness a student uprising against that regime, which fails, resulting in Russia's tighter grip. You hear about people leaving your homeland, and you see no reason you shouldn't. You are alone anyway — you might as well be alone in a better place.

And you know that God will always be with you.

After a train ride which takes you just outside the border zone, you hike twenty snow-drenched, yet moonlit miles into Austria, first escaping Hungarian guards, then machine guns, finally spotted by Austrian searchlights, beaming their welcome. That morning, when you see oranges and bananas, you begin to taste freedom. You haven't seen such exotic delicacies since your childhood. After several stops first at your uncle's in Vienna where he helps you begin to adjust, then to barracks where you learn about the ways of the New World—you board a plane for America.

There, under a blue sky, across a vast expanse of land, you take a journey you could have never imagined a year before. With sponsors, you learn English, you find work. With the bidding of your new American wife, you return to college and earn a teaching degree in German and History. Your son is born and you move your family to Colorado, where you teach at a high school. Your daughter is born, and you live a long, happy, prosperous life, serving the Lord.

You take a trip with your wife, back in time, to Hungary, to see the battered buildings, your once-beautiful home, and sad yet grateful that you escaped that life. Now, forty years later, you face old age and more hardship. Yet God still guides you. Perhaps He told you to write this book. It is your way of thanking Him, of reaching out once more, sharing with others how they can survive almost anything with God's help. You know, because you did.

George Neuvirth, author of Out of Hungary: A Memoir, has lived this life. He does not lament the past, nor judge those around him who complain without cause. Instead, he wants his readers to know that true freedom is in Christ. The Lord frees us from our hate, our grudges, and our resentments, so we can receive His blessings. He promises us Eternal Life. Yet while on this Earth, Jesus Christ gives us a reason to live, the peace we all strive for, and the love we all need.

In the Beginning. . .

— a little bit of Hungarian history

Budapest could glisten in the summer afternoon sunshine, like Constantinople (Istanbul) with its multiple steeples. Ah! Budapest, the Pearl of the Danube, the Paris of the East. The style of the city was Baroque, the style of the powerful, rich, and pompous, the style of the Habsburg Empire, the Austrians. Budapest women were well and tastefully dressed, as were the men. The Bohemian lifestyle, unconventional and easygoing, showed up in cafes rich with good food and Gypsies, playing their violins before the tables into the early morning hours. But that was the capital of Hungary before World War II . . .

The Danube River divides Budapest between "Buda" and "Pest" and is spanned by beautiful bridges. The most historic of these bridges, the "Chain Bridge," was built by the Hungarian aristocrat, Szechenyi, in 1848. The river flows majestically through the quay, banks masterfully reinforced with stone on either side. Budapesters still love to wander along the wharf for hours on warm summer evenings.

The Romans called the river "Danubius." It starts in Germany in the Black Forest and ends, after a seventeen-hundred-mile journey, at the Black Sea in Romania. Eight countries are washed by its waters, and ancient settlements—more than eight thousand years old—have been discovered along its banks. Attila the Hun, the Turks, and the Romans all sailed along its course. For the Gypsies, the Danube was the "Dustless Road."

Legend has it that somewhere in the Danube near Budapest, Attila—the great king of the Huns—is buried in three caskets. One iron, one silver, and one gold—one inside the other. During World War II, the Hungarian government explored the bottom of the river in different spots, but they found nothing. History tries to classify Attila as a Hungarian king because he once had his court at the old Buda fortress, from where he raided Western Europe. Many Hungarians are named Attila.

Budapest and Hungary had always been the bridge between East and West. Hordes of invaders in the past as well as modern armies clashed there: the Mongols, the Tartars, the Turks, the Austrians, the Germans, and the Russians. Budapest, like other European capitals, has often been destroyed in its thousand-year history.

The Hungarian tongue does not have an Indo-European background as most languages. Instead, its background is Finno-Ugric. The Hungarians actually came from the Russian steppes. Turkish nomads roamed with them, giving their language some Turkish words as well.

Seven original tribes make up the Hungarian people. Arpad was their first leader. He led them into the Carpathian Basin, the fertile valleys surrounded by the snow-covered peaks of the Transylvanian Alps, which would later become Hungary. The tribes often made raids into Western Europe, Austria, and Germany. For many years people prayed, "Almighty God, save us from the Magyars [Hungarians]." Then at the Battle of Lechfeld in 955 AD near Augsburg in Bavaria, they were defeated for good by the German king, Otto I. They had to stay within their territory, and those they had once conquered showed them how to settle down from a belligerent to an agrarian life.

Then Stephan I, Arpad's grandson, wanted to Christianize Hungary. He sent for a crown from Pope Sylvester I for his coronation, around 1000 AD. The top of the crown has a cross, bent sometime during its many journeys, which kept it from danger when foreign armies looted and robbed its homeland. The crown was at risk the last time during the Hungarian Revolution, in 1956. It was spirited to the United States for safekeeping until President Nixon sent it back during his term (1969 — 1974). Now it is displayed in the National Museum with other regalia, where school children can observe and study it.

Hungarian kings as well as foreign kings would sit on the throne of St. Stephan. In the thirteenth century, the Ottoman (Turkish) Empire conquered Europe from the East up to Vienna, while the Moors conquered Spain from the West, from North Africa.

In 1526, the Ottoman Sultan Suleiman I the Magnificent, wanted to conquer Austria. He asked permission to enter Southern Hungary, but his request was denied. The young Hungarian king, Louis II, wanted to meet the Sultan and his troops head-on. They met at the Battle of Mohacs. The Sultan had two hundred thousand troops; the Hungarians, only twenty-six thousand. The young Hungarian king hoped that John I Zapolya, a Hungarian aristocrat who would later take the throne himself, would come to his aid with his fifty thousand men. But he had made a separate agreement with the Turks.

The disunity of the Hungarian people started to reveal itself at this point in history. As the battle began, the Turks feigned retreat and the Hungarians were on their heels. All at once, the retreating Turkish lines opened up and massacred the Hungarian troops with their cannons. The young king perished as he jumped a creek, and his horse buried him underneath.

Hungary then became partitioned into Imperial Hungary, Turkish-occupied Hungary, and Transylvania, a Vassal State protected by, but subjected to Hungary's rule. This situation remained from 1526 to 1684 when the Austrians pushed the Turks back for good, as they tried to conquer Vienna.

From then on, the Hungarian nobility chose a Habsburg emperor from Austria to sit on the Hungarian throne. Hungary was not really independent. Quasi-independence came in 1867 through the Compromise, an agreement that ushered in the "Dual Monarchy" of Austria-Hungary. This was a unique but excellent geopolitical setup. The Empire was divided between Austria and Hungary. A little river flowing south from Vienna, the Leitha, was the boundary. Everything west of it was under Austrian domain, everything east of it, Hungarian.

They were two independent countries with parliaments in Budapest and Vienna. But there were three common ministries:

Foreign Affairs, Finances, and Defense. The so-called "Delega-tion," delegates from each parliament, coordinated the com-mon affairs of the two countries. These governing factors made Hungary a quasi world power, and a good place to live.

The family name, Habsburg, is derived from two words, "Habicht" and "Burg," or hawk's nest. In the 1200's, the Aus-trian family had a fort in Switzerland called Habichtsburg, later translated into Habsburg. Slowly but surely, the family spread all over Europe, not waging many wars, but intermarrying with the different royal families of Europe instead. In this way, they added and added to their holdings until almost every European country was under their authority.

The Habsburgs were extremely "rank conscious" and their court was very formal, heavy, and cold. In the "Burg," the Im-perial Palace in Vienna, everyone had a different door to enter or exit according to rank. In parades, those who were not dukes or archdukes had to stay behind. Even in death, a casket would be lower or higher according to one's status.

The last emperor who took his "by the grace of God" rule seriously was Francis Joseph. He slept on an iron bed as did Napoleon. Likewise, he was one of the longest-ruling monarchs in history, from 1848 to 1916—sixty-eight years.

Once a year, Francis Joseph went out to the Prater, the Vi-enna amusement park, to be among his people. He never had a bodyguard with him and often appeared at the court's balls. He had a good heart. Once he found a bug in his bread and wanted to fire the cook. Someone discouraged him from this and he let the cook stay.

The emperor, however, was not spared personal tragedy. He had four brothers. One, Maximilian, was made emperor of Mex-ico by Emperor Napoleon III and his French army. Two years later, Benito Juarez gained control of Mexico and had Maximil-ian executed. Francis Joseph's son, Rudolph, committed suicide. And the emperor's wife, Empress Elizabeth, the most beautiful woman in Europe at that time, was murdered by an Italian "ir-redenta," a nationalist.

In November, 1916, in the middle of World War I, he asked his Hungarian Aid de Camp, Count Parr, to wake him early in the morning because he had much to do. He was found dead in his bed the next day at eighty-two years old. This way he was spared the dissolution of his Empire that came two years later.

When Rudolph, his only son, committed suicide, the heir apparent became another brother who did not want the throne, rejecting it in favor of his son (Francis Joseph's nephew) Francis Ferdinand. The young man was rude, quick-tempered, and did not like the Hungarians, which created tension because the Compromise of 1867 had made Hungarians and Austrians equal partners.

Ferdinand wanted to bring some other nationalities, such as the Bohemians and Moravians, into the federation of Austria and Hungary as equals. But the Hungarians fought it. As "political pushers," assertive and strong Nationals, they did not want any other nationalities to join the Dual Monarchy. They had accepted the alliance with Austria for only one reason, its strength against defeat.

In 1908, Austria and Hungary formally annexed the Turkish province of Bosnia-Heregovina. It is one of the Balkan countries, others being the former Yugoslavia and Bulgaria. All had been under the Ottoman Empire's rule for centuries. "Austria-Hungary. . .demonstrated that they could rule just as viciously as the Turks. . .in fact, the wealth of Vienna and Budapest was built on the broken backs of their Slav subjects."[1]

Bosnia-Heregovina' s population consisted in part of Serbs, who started the idea of assassination as a means of shaking and ridding themselves of foreign domination. They considered themselves part of the Turkish Empire, and to go from that life to one under Habsburg rule wrought quite a change in culture as well as form of government.

In 1914, the governor general of Serbia, Potiorek, invited Ferdinand to oversee military maneuvers. Not wanting to seem

---

1   Kaplan, Robert D., *Balkan Ghosts, A Journey Through History* (New York: Vintage Books, a Division of Random House, Inc., 1993).

rude, he accepted. As Inspector General, Ferdinand could take his wife, Sophie, with him. The two were in a "morganatic" marriage, a Greek word meaning "below rank." She had to follow her husband in parades, and her casket would be displayed lower than his at their funeral. But when he served as the head of the armed forces, she could be at his side.

He chose a dangerous time to go—June 28, St. Vitus Day, the day in 1389 AD when the Slavs lost a battle against the Turks. It "became a symbol of all Serbian struggles for freedom."[2] Austria-Hungary knew about this sensitive day, and they knew about the Black Hand, a terrorist group who had plans to assassinate Ferdinand. Authorities warned the couple not to go, but to no avail.

They left two young boys (who were to play a role in politics after World War II) and a girl at Konopischt, their country palace in Bohemia. The first assassination attempt happened during the trip to the Mayor's office. The would-be assassin, Cabrinovic, aimed for the Archduke's green feathers, but the bomb bounced off of the car. Ferdinand was furious. He told the mayor he had come with good intentions, but was awaited with bombs. Yet the mayor still let him give his speech.[3][4]

After the speech and dinner, the chauffeur was told to take another route to the Governor's Palace. The retinue (entourage) came to a fork in the road and the chauffeur slowed down. In the crowd stood one of the assassins, Princip. He ran toward the car and pulled the trigger on his pistol. This time, the attempt succeeded. Francis Ferdinand was heard to say, "It is nothing, Sophie, stay alive for our children." Both died within an hour.

For two weeks, nothing happened between the two foreign

---

2   Brook-Shepherd, *Gordan, Archduke of Sarajevo, the Romance and Tragedy of Franz Ferdinand of Austria* (Boston • Toronto: Little, Brown and Company, 1984).

3   "Today the old Austrian town hall is the University Library. The broad steps outside, which the Archduke and his wife descended to make the last brief drive to their deaths, are dotted with students."

4   Ibid.

ministries. Several of the conspirators were hanged, but Princip could not be shot because of his age. He soon died of tuberculosis, not aware of what he had unleashed.[5] [6] Before long, the world would be in flames.

---

5 "Princip, the assassin, is now Princip the national hero. Where he fired the two bullets there [is] an impression of his feet [in] a concrete slab."

6 Ibid.

Important
Twentieth-Century Dates:

- June 28, 1914 — Archduke Francis Ferdinand of Austria is murdered with his wife Sophie in Sarajevo.
- July, 1914 — World War I breaks out.
- 1918 — World War I ends.
- 1919 — The Versailles Peace Treaty: Germany and Hungary lose two-thirds of their territories.[7]
- 1919 — The Weimar Republic, where democracy and arts flourish, is established in Germany.
- January, 1923 — French and Belgian forces occupy Germany's main industrial region, the Ruhr, claiming that Germany had defaulted on reparation deliveries.
- January 30, 1933 — Hitler comes to power, legally. He declares the Versailles Peace Treaty null, and starts arming right under the nose of the Western Powers.
- 1936 — Germany's reoccupation of its industrial area.
- March, 1938 — Germany annexes Austria.
- September, 1938 — Munich Pact: Sudetenland, the German-speaking part of Czecholslovakia, is relinquished to Germany.
- March, 1939 — Germany occupies all of Czechoslovakia, making it a German protectorate.
- September, 1939 — World War II breaks out.
- 1941 — Hungary comes into the war on the side of Germany, the Axis Powers.
- March 19, 1944 — Germany occupies Hungary.

---

7   When Lloyd George, the British negotiator, went home, he commented that there would be another war in twenty years. He was right.

- October 15, 1944 — The Hungarian Nazis, the Arrow Cross, take over Hungary.
- Christmas, 1944 — The Siege of Budapest.
- May, 1945 -- Hungary loses World War II.
- 1945 – 1990 — The Russian occupation of Hungary.
- October — November, 1956 — The Hungarian Revolution.

Signs of the Times. . .

— a childhood on the brink

In the summer days of 1939, I was a childish and naive thirteen-year-old boy. The hard life had not touched me yet. But I often had a feeling that my abundant life would not last, which I was to discover soon. I never told my parents about my premonitions. . .

My father said, "Today, the war broke out." It was September 1, 1939. I was an only child, born in Budapest, Hungary. My parents were wealthy and influential. Two weeks before, we had returned from Switzerland to our house on a hill overlooking Budapest.

In 1937, while we were in Switzerland, our whole household had been moved from the Pest side, to the Buda side on the hill. Upon our return, my clothes were in the drawers and the books were on the shelves in exactly the same order they had been before.

In our new home, the maid and cook each had their own room. The gardener and his family had an apartment in the basement. We had the most beautiful view of Budapest. We could see the Royal Palace and some of the buildings, which housed the various government ministries.

For several summers, my parents had left me in Switzerland to learn French. I always stayed with families who had children. In 1939, I stayed with a pastor's family. Once, we children were caught smoking in the tree house, and the pastor's wife tied us up in bed without supper as punishment.

The village was high in the mountains, above Lausanne, in the French-speaking part of Switzerland. We played in the gorgeous alpine forests and took long walks to collect snails or blueberries. This area was known for people with bone tuberculosis.

They stayed in sanitariums and we'd see them walking around without a nose or ear, or some other ailment.

The Swiss love their mountains. Once the pastor took us on a big trip to a glacier. We had to be roped together for the climb, and then we slept in a mountain youth cabin. I also saw the new movie, Heidi, that summer.

We had to ring the church bells every Sunday before the service. Church bells are not easy to ring; you not only have to know how to start the big ones, but how to stop them. This particular church bell was small and we had no problem with it. But the night before the Sunday church service, we had to clean the pews, and as it got dark, the scene became eerie.

Then in August,1939, there were rumors that the war might break out at any moment. Foreigners left Switzerland quickly, as everyone wanted to get home. I was on the last train that would cross the border into Hungary. We were going through Vienna on our way to Budapest. Sitting across from me was the heiress to the Herz Salami Corporation.[8] She was crying, no doubt because she was Jewish. I never saw or heard of her again. Perhaps like other Jewish families, hers was able to bribe the Nazis. But not many were successful.

When we arrived in Vienna, red swastika flags were draped three stories high on the buildings. Hitler had made Austria part of Germany, calling it Ostland. Soon our train arrived in Budapest. It was a lovely day, the weather was calm, and no one in the world suspected what was coming, at least not many in Hungary.

As we sat around the table waiting to be served, my father's words hung in the air. The maid came in to serve the meal, with the required apron around her waist and a small lace cap on her head. My mother was always served first, as were all housewives in Europe, then my father, then myself.

The meal consisted of soup, the main course, and then dessert. The meat had to be extremely tender, and when the cake was extra good, the cook was complemented and congratulated.

---

8   Herz is a winter salami that is still a Hungarian specialty.

My father served as a high-ranking secretary in the Defense Department, where personal titles and ranks were very important and highly sought after. This was especially true in Hungary, Austria, and Germany. Titles and ranks were used to such a degree that there is no clear description of them in other languages. Even the children had titles, all with certain responsibilities and privileges. Later, I remember addressing professors in Law school as "Your Excellency."

My father was in Vienna during one of his many trips. He was eating at the Hotel Sacher. At a neighboring table sat a lovely lady. He passed the salt to her and they started talking. She would become my mother.

My father had inherited a sawmill, in the midst of the great oak forests, from my grandfather. It was seven hundred miles from Budapest. My father made oak flooring, which he shipped to different countries. One of my treasured memories is a letter my father wrote to my mother from the sawmill. In it he tells her to take care of herself and rest because she was pregnant at that time with me. My arrival was greatly anticipated.

As Budapest was the Paris of the East with its fashion and culture, so Vienna was the center of a world empire. Vienna had the best surgeons, the greatest musicians, and the foremost politicians. It led in fashion and art for several centuries. The Hotel Sacher was a famous gathering place for the rich, kings and queens, and even spies.

Its most famous dish was the Sacher torte, a multilayer chocolate cake, which is still the hotel's specialty. Another well-known multilayer chocolate cake is the Dobos torte, named after the Hungarian chef of the mighty king, Mathias, the great emperor of the eighteenth century.

I was born premature and weighed very little. Our family pediatrician came to the house, picking me up like a package and putting me on a scale. My mother was horrified, but he told her not to worry, that I would develop into a strong boy. He was a personal family friend, as was our lawyer and other wealthy people.

At the age of four, I became very ill. I fell down and although I ran right to my parents, the wound developed an infection that spread through my body. All at once, I became very listless, and nobody knew what was wrong. I couldn't explain it. My pediatrician told us we had one more chance for me to survive, by calling on a surgeon who was arriving from Vienna that same evening.

Our doctor went to the station to meet the train. The next day, the famous Viennese surgeon examined me, pointed near my kidney and said to our doctor, "Here we have to cut." They operated on me and saved my life. One more day and I would have died. About eighteen years later, I realized this as the first indication that God had a plan for me. He had stepped into my life.

Then when I was nine years old, my doctor discovered that I had a slight case of tuberculosis, so I was sent to a sanitarium in the Austrian Alps. All the beds were rolled out onto a long terrace. We had to stay there all the time for the fresh air, day and night, winter and summer. Often on winter mornings, we would brush the snow from our pillows and blankets, and ourselves. I stayed there for nine months, continuing with my schooling.

At that time, we lived on the Pest side of Budapest. Pest is the east side and flat, while Buda is the west side and hilly. We occupied two floors in a three-story house on a corner. Thick carpets, hanging down from tracks, divided the rooms, and expensive paintings by Hungarian and other famous artists hung everywhere. They did not hang on nails or hooks but on wires because of their weight. Museums and art galleries often showed my father's collection.

We had tile stoves in each room. The richer the family, the more elaborate the tile stove. I remember the servants stuffing each stove with wood on cold winter mornings. The rooms were about fifteen feet tall and hard to heat. In front of our home were beautiful chestnut trees that would bloom each May with candle-like blooms, bright red and orange, and white. They shaded some of our windows in the summer Chestnut trees grow forty feet high in every European capital.

For a while, my grandmother on my father's side lived with

us. She died in 1930, when I was four, so I don't remember her well. Four or six horses pulled her casket at her funeral. This was a symbol of our wealth and high status because the higher up, the more horses were used: two for a commoner, four for a baron or count, six for a prince, and eight for royalty.

My father loved his mother very much and he often told me that the love of parents is a blessing in a child's life. How true! Even the scriptures say, *"Honor your father and mother . . . that it may go well with you and that you may enjoy long life on the earth."* (Eph. 6:2-3 NIV) The blessing of honoring one's parents brings peace to one's life.

My grandfather on my father's side must have been Saxon by decent. The Saxons were a fine German tribe that moved to Translyvania. Some of them moved into a pure Hungarian settlement in the north of Hungary. I know that my grandfather was a stern disciplinarian as well as very influential. He was on the board of the Vienna Credit Institute, one of Europe's finest banks.

My mother was Viennese and her parents were merchants. They had a leather goods store on the Graben, the fifth avenue of Vienna. When Emperor Francis Joseph rebuilt the city, the city ended at the Graben, which means "ditch." But when the walls came down that were around the city, the Graben became the fifth avenue.

The Austrians were a happy and easygoing people, traits that spilled into their "schlamperei," or sloppiness. There were no regular working hours. For example, one could go to the office at nine o'clock or nine-thirty and leave at two. But my mother was anything but sloppy. She was a fine housewife and cook, even though she had a maid and a cook. She had to manage a big household and satisfy father's punctuality and critical taste. Lunch was served at two o'clock, but I was already home from school by then. Supper was always at seven o'clock sharp.

My life was content. I had everything, yet I was not spoiled. The war was far away, even in the late 1930's. The Budapest hills where we later lived were beautiful playgrounds, with their dusty roads and chestnut trees, where the cuckoo bird sang every afternoon. I would approach its sound, but it would always stop singing, so I would never know from what tree or branch it chirped its melody. It was that elusive.

My friends and I would bicycle or play Indians in those hills, undisturbed. There was no traffic in the countryside. There was no bus going up the hill towards our house in the 1930's or '40's, so we had to walk. It took us about twenty minutes from the streetcar stop. I often ran up and down the whole stretch three or four times a day.

I spent my four elementary school years in a German school. One of my teachers was Herr Kurz, meaning "short," but he was six-feet, five-inches tall. After elementary school, I was enrolled in a "gymnasium." This word in Europe means high school, not a large room for sports and exercise. These schools were segregated, not according to race but to sex. I went to an all-boy school with all male teachers. Girls went to all-girl schools with all female teachers.

In America, the students move from room to room, but in Hungary, the teachers would change rooms, although we did have a homeroom teacher, the same one for about six years. Our school day was from eight o'clock to one o'clock.

At ten, we had fifteen minutes of pause to eat our "uzsona," a snack that we brought from home. Also, unlike American schools, we had school on Saturday.

There were not many discipline problems because if one moved around just a little more than usual, a note was sent home for his father to sign. When this happened to me, I did everything to have my mother sign my note because she was more lenient. My father went to most of the teacher conferences as my mother had difficulty speaking Hungarian, which is not an easy language

I would talk to my father in Hungarian and then turn to my mother and speak in German. This would make it possible for me to teach German in America twenty-five years later. How thankful I am to my mother for her gift of a second language.

Because German was her native tongue, my mother would meet with my German teacher, who usually told her that he couldn't give me a good grade since I didn't prepare my homework, although he knew I was the best student in the class.

Our homework was demanding. I ate lunch when I came

home from school, but then I could do nothing else but home-work. My father would often come into my room to question me on my lessons. If I was not prepared, I had to study more, sometimes late into the night until he was convinced that I knew my lessons.

I was weak in math so my parents got me a tutor. Three times a week, my piano and French teachers came to the house, both ladies. I could only play after all my lessons and home-work were finished. I had to play pieces on the piano for my parents to show how advanced I was. It was exciting for me, but I also worried about making a mistake. We were perfectionists, which does not always serve one well in life.

Almost every night in the winter, our chauffeur would take me to the ice rink at the city park, where I played hockey with peers. I never returned to the rink when World War II ended and Communism took over. Somehow, I thought ice- skating was a Capitalistic sport, perhaps because I had played with rich children before and the Communists despised us.

During my high school years, we often spent Christmas vacation skiing in Badgastein, Austria, a resort town for the rich and famous, where kings and politicians came to "take the waters." Arriving at the train station, the guests were taken by horse-drawn sleighs to the hotel. The sky twinkled with thou-sands of little stars, and the snow cracked under the sleigh. It was a winter paradise. It was there I fell in love for the first time, at eleven-years-old. I met Rosemary, an Austrian my own age, on the ski slopes.

But I also remember some Nazi officers verbally attacking the Jewish manager of the hotel. In the late 1930's, Jews were be-ing sent away from Germany and Austria. They called it "Zim-merrein," the clearing-out the "pest of Jews."

And Nation Shall Rise Against Nation. . .

— a country caught in the middle

> In Germany, the Nazis came for the Communists and I did not speak up, because I was not a Communist. Then they came for the Jews and I did not speak up, because I was not a Jew. Then they came for the Labor Unionists and I did not speak up, because I was not a Labor Unionist. Then they came for the Catholics and I was a Protestant, so I did not speak up. Then they came for me. By that time there was no one to speak up anymore for me.
>
> —Martin Niemoelle (1892 – 1984)
> Lutheran Bishop of Berlin

What can be blamed for the collapse of Germany, for the many atrocities that were committed? Its geographical location? The regime, the government? Its character that changed colors with the wind? A segment of the populous, or the whole population? There were several elements behind Germany's downfall, including the cooperation of its citizens. People in general knew what was going on. They saw it on the streets, in the stores, in buildings, and in restaurants . . .[9]

This picture would repeat itself in Budapest. Crowds would watch as Jews were herded by the brick factories, in the November rain and mud. The manager of my father's sawmill was

---

9 Goldhagen, Daniel Jonah, *Hitler's Willing Executioners, Ordinary Germans and the Holocaust* (New York: Vintage Books, a Division of Random House, Inc., 1996).

Jewish and his whole family perished in an extermination camp. I read the last letter he wrote to my father. My father's lawyer and his wife died the same horrible way. They said good-bye to their daughter before going to the gas chamber. She survived, but alone, with no family, she was seen weeping in front of a store.

My mother was of Jewish descent, which was not a problem until Germany and its persecution of Jews in the 1930's and '40's. She was in danger of deportation and possible death. I remember her coming into my room and asking me if I would mind being Jewish. I said I would. Oh, how I must have broken her heart.

But this was the view at that time in most European countries. The Jews were no good. They represented shame. They needed to be eradicated. Later, when I accepted Christ as my Personal Saviour, I learned that the people of Israel are the "chosen ones," the "apple of God's eye," and it is not a shame to be Jewish, but actually a blessing. Actually, every born-again Christian belongs to the "spiritual Israel." He is a Jew by heart.

My mother would be so pleased to know how I would answer her question now, but it took a complete turnaround, a conversion of my heart through Jesus Christ.

That September of 1939, we had to take our family papers to a military office for identification. The Nuremberg Laws, two constitutional laws issued in 1935 at a special session of the Reichstag, the German parliament, demanded that there be no Jewish blood in a citizen, going back to both sets of grandparents. Jewish blood became the basis for further legal exclusion of Jews from German life.

The first Nuremberg Law, the Reich Citizenship Law, stated that only Germans could be citizens of the Reich. Along with thirteen complimentary ordinances passed from 1933 to 1943, the Jews lost their political, social, and economic rights. The second Nuremberg Law was for the protection of German blood and honor. It prohibited marriages between Jews and Germans, as well as extramarital intercourse between the two races.

When I brought our family papers to a military office, the officer commented that my father's so-called Aryan blood saved me from being a Jew. Aryan was both a race and a language. The notion of an Aryan race rose during the nineteenth century. Aryans, those who spoke Indo-European languages, were considered superior to Jews, Arabs, Asians, and Africans.

This idea was propagated by the French count, Gobineau, and later by his disciple, Englishman Houston Chamberlain. The Nordic (Germanic) people came to be regarded as the purest Aryans. Adolph Hitler would seize this belief that the Indo-Europeans, or Indo-Aryans, and their languages, were superior. And he would make it the basis of German government policies.

But all this had nothing to do with Jewish blood or purity of race. The Germans distinguishing a difference between pure and impure blood was a Satanic deception. There is no such thing as a superior race. It does not exist. Instead, Hitler imposed German mythology into everyday life. The German blond and blue-eyed boy and the rolled-up-hair virgin figures of Goethe (a German dramatist) were only prototypes of German Aryanism. It became fanaticism, an uneducated, narrow-minded view that led to cruelty, murder, destruction, and the collapse of everything decent.

Yet narrow-minded thugs governed all of Europe for many years in the 1930's and '40's. As with Germany, almost every country had their own stamp of Nazism: Hungary had the Arrow Cross; Latvia, the Thunder Cross; and Romania, its Iron Guard. They all wooed Germany's favor, even trying to outdo the German fanaticism.

In March, 1941, Hitler invaded Yugoslavia and the Hungarian Regent, Nicholas Horthy, agreed to cooperate with Germany in an armed attack, even though Hungary had signed a treaty of "eternal friendship" with Yugoslavia only a few months earlier. The great Prime Minister, Count Teleky, descended from an old Hungarian family, committed suicide, but left a note to Horthy concerning the "eternal friendship" with Yugoslavia:

> Your Serene Highness! We betrayed our words, the word in our treaty of eternal peace that was based on your speech . . . the nation is aware of it, and we disregarded her honor. We have sided with the scoundrels. We will become despoilers of corpses—the lowliest of all nations. . .[10]

After reading the note, Horthy immediately wrote to Hitler, accepting the new "spoils" from him:

> I do not doubt that Your Excellency will understand that this tragic case has deeply shaken me . . . in accordance with my letter of March 28, 1941, we have already taken military measures . . .[11]

Hungary saw the chance to "reconquest" some of the territories lost at the Versailles Peace Treaty in 1919, for example, parts of Yugoslavia. Hence, some Hungarians were committed to support the German cause. It was a manifestation of national gratitude towards Germany. So Horthy meant well, but his policies were uncertain, hesitant, and of dire consequences, because they got Hungary involved on the Axis side.

Horthy was sent to the Russian Front, but his father, and Prime Minister Kallay had given orders that he was not "to be used." After all, the upper and lower houses of parliament had just appointed him Deputy Regent. Such a high-ranking person could not be exposed to dangerous situations. Likewise, President Charles de Gaulle of France did not allow the modern

---

10 Szinai, Miklós and László Szücs, editors. *The Confidential Papers of Admiral Horthy* (Budapest: Corvina Press, 1965).

11 Ibid.

lineage of Napoleon Bonaparte to be thrown into combat. His bloodline had to be protected.

However, young Horthy disobeyed orders. He went up in an Italian plane that crashed, and lost his life. Whether the plane was faulty, sabotaged by the Germans, or Horthy was to blame, we will never know. In any case, he left behind a young widow, a six-year-old son, and a whole country in mourning. As it is here in America, the color of mourning in Europe is black. However, there, the funeral announcements are framed in black, funeral parlors are draped in black, and the mourners wear black armbands for a year.

As the war came closer to Hungary, its pace was slow at first. Air raids became more frequent. They started at ten o'clock p.m., interrupting the news. The British bombed us during the day, and the Americans attacked at night. After North Africa was retaken from the Germans, and the Sicily landing, the Allied Forces established bases in Italy. So their targets became closer and easier to reach. Often I went to school with sleepy eyes after a night of bombing.

Some teachers were called into the army and sent to the Russian Front. Being sent to the Russian Front was actually a form of punishment. A great number of men disappeared on the vast Russian steppes and tundra, never to be heard from again. In 1943, at the Battle of Stalingrad, the most decisive battle in the Second World War, thousands of German soldiers were captured. By 1956, fourteen years later, only three thousand men had trickled back.

That winter of 1942 to 43, was one of the most severe during the war. We children had "szenszunet" (coal vacation) from school for three months, because the coal was needed for military transports. I remember spending part of my days building caves in the snow in our yard. Yet we still finished the school year on time.

Most of Hungary was for a German victory. My father was not, being upper middle class, and of course the Jews were against Germany. My father had said at the beginning of the war, in 1939, that Germany would lose. But who would have predicted this when Germany, with its "Blitzkrieg" (lightning-type warfare) was so successful on every front. Even Pope Pius XII rooted for a German victory because he feared Communism so much more.[12]

Some teachers were also rooting for a German victory, partly because they were anti-Semitic. I remember how one of my best friends, who was Jewish, was humiliated by a teacher and had to stand in the corner during class. This boy came from a very wealthy English textile family. He would later perish by freezing to death in a concentration camp.

We listened to the news everyday. We had to sit close to the radio because the Nazis, and later the Russians, would jam the airwaves. It became a skill to clear the shortwave channels. Sometimes we could find out how things stood at the frontlines. For instance, the Germans would broadcast from North Africa. But all at once, that particular station would go silent, meaning that the Germans had left that area, one way or another.

The main station to listen to was the English BBC, three short and one long sign. But one day we were ordered to give up our radios and take them to the city hall. The Germans did not want us to listen to enemy broadcasts. It is intriguing, though, that after the war, we were able to find and retrieve our own radios among thousands of others. At the same time, almost all of our other possessions were gone, vanished.

Because an air raid could come at anytime, the radios were always on in both homes and offices. There were three stages of aid raids:

---

12 Excellent works on this are Pius XII and the Third Reich, by Saul Friedländer, and La Popessa, by Paul I. Murphy. The latter concerns a brilliant nun who wielded power by being the Pope's aid, housekeeper, confidante, and advisor. She never understood why the Pope did not speak up against the Germans during all of the war years.

Friedländer, Saul, *Pius XII and the Third Reich, a Documentation* (New York: Alfred A. Knoff, 1966).

Murphy, Paul I., *La Popessa, the Controversial Biography of Sister Pascalina, the Most Powerful Woman in Vatican History* (New York: Warner Books, 1983).

1. When the radio said "disturbance flight, disturbance flight," enemy planes had crossed the border or one plane was in the vicinity.
2. "Air danger, air danger" meant many planes were approaching the capital or any other place.
3. "Air raid, air raid" warned us that ten minutes remained before bombing.

In the downtown district, it was obligatory to go into basements. In outlying areas, we could do as we wanted. Everyone could make up his own mind My family always had a suitcase ready and would go down into our basement, but only when the action got too rough. There were always blackouts, everywhere. We had black curtains on our windows, and the cars had "hoods" over the headlights with two-inch slits in them. One could not even smoke a cigarette during an air raid, because the light could be seen ten thousand feet up.

When the air raid sirens went silent, within ten minutes we could hear a distant roar. One plane, just one plane, would approach the target area. This plane dropped so-called "Stalin candles" over the target area. These were torches on parachutes that slowly came down, giving off a yellowish, eerie light, but one so bright you could read by it. After a few minutes, we could hear another roar and then the planes would come, wave after wave.

As they reached a certain line, the flack from our Boforz cannons would shoot up and we could see tracers by the hundreds. At the same time, dozens of strong beams would crisscross the sky. I would often see a plane caught in one and then tracers coming from every direction, going after it. Once, during a midday raid, I saw at least two-hundred planes in the sky.

In the countryside, when the peasants heard that a pilot had been shot down, they took their pitch forks and ran in the direction where the plane had landed, or crashed. For six years, my teen years, my most impressive years, I lived with blackouts and air raids. When peace would finally come, I would not know anymore what that meant.

Meanwhile, my high school graduation grew near. The year

was 1944, which I call the "Deep War Year." We went through things that only happen "once in a thousand years." But of course we could not see ahead. Only God knows the future, and the eventual good that comes out of all circumstances.

High school graduation was different in Hungary than in America. At the end of our studies, we took both oral and written tests, which lasted for days. During some of the written tests, we would be interrupted by sirens and go down to the bunker or basement. After the "all clear" sounded, we left our papers behind and went home. The teachers used what they had to grade us.

For oral exams, five or six of us would sit before a committee, answering questions in almost every subject. We received a separate graduation certificate for each subject. I had taken six years of Latin, which I hated but passed. Later, I used it to teach foreign languages.

Our graduation banquet was served in a restaurant. I don't remember any teachers showing up. They were all gone. Some were fighting the enemy, the Russians or Americans. My parents gave me a watch for a graduation present. I already had a watch, so I put one on each wrist and showed them off.

Back in my junior year, my parents had given me a more expensive watch. Somehow I left it in my gym class and it was stolen. That day after school, I was scared to go home. I went to the Principal, who was a relative, and told him, "I cannot go home." Of course, I eventually did, but my father did not talk to me much for a day or two. This was not punishment, rather a natural reaction. I was more upset than my parents. I was a good boy. I always wanted to please my parents and never would have done anything to sadden them.

A House Divided
Against Itself. . .

— a treacherous turning point

I have a stamp with the date 1904 – 1942 on it. On it is a picture of a handsome pilot surrounded by planes, and horsemen representing the legendary Magyars who occupied Hungary in 800 AD. The background is black, the sign and color of mourning. The handsome pilot is Stephen Horthy, the eldest of two sons of the Regent Nicholas Horthy, who came to power in 1919. He was the Commander of the Austro-Hungarian Navy and Aid de Camp to Emperor Frances Joseph. His title was "Your Highness." His regency was to end when Hungary would choose again to have a king. It is interesting that Hungary in the 1920's, '30's, and '40's had an admiral as the head of state, yet no sea. It was a kingdom without a king. . .

A Fuhrer (Hitler) top secret directive was issued under the "Geheime Staatspolizei" (Gestapo), explaining why Germany would invade Hungary: 1) Hungary's Prime Minister's (Kallay) negotiations, 2) the dominating influence of the Jews in Hungary, and 3) the corrupt element of the Hungarian aristocracy. This military action would be called "Margarethe."

Hungary's Regent, Horthy, received an invitation from Hitler to visit him on March 15, 1944, at Klessheim Castle in Bavaria. He arrived on March 18, but when he wanted to leave, his dagger was taken from him and he was detained. Hitler achieved his aim, depriving Hungary of leadership. The next day, on March 19, 1944, the Germans invaded Hungary.

It was an overcast day and planes were flying overhead. I was practicing my piano lesson as usual. It must have been a

Sunday because the Germans would start operations on Sunday, when people were more relaxed and tended to be resting. I continued playing the piano, oblivious that since the early morning hours the Gestapo had already been rounding up political figures of the Left. The Germans would always begin in the early hours of the morning, finding people in their deepest sleep, less prepared and alert.

The Kallay administration resigned their authority that same day in March. The only resistance seemed to come from one member of parliament, Bajczy Zsilinsky. When a Gestapo detachment drove up in front of his apartment, he greeted them with pistol shots. He was arrested and freed, but arrested again. On December 24, 1944, the Germans executed him.

Prime Minister Kallay heard the gun shots, as he had also been arrested and put in the same prison. On one of the main streets in Budapest, there is a plaque in remembrance of what he said: "Let the Hungarians in the future have more character and spine." The old aristocratic Hungarian regime, which had held for many centuries, had fallen.

I remember seeing Gestapo motorized vehicles stopping before buildings to take people away. The Hungarian army offered not even a token resistance. There is considerable disagreement as to whether any shots were fired at all.[13] Not only did the German occupation forces encounter no resistance from the Hungarian army, but neither did the population resist.

For a while, nothing really changed. My father continued to work on his beautiful rose garden. Our cook, an elderly lady, still cooked; the maid served the meals and cleaned; and the caretaker worked on the lawn. Our yard was full of flowering bushes. The garage was at the end of the yard, and a lovely pine-laden walk was between it and the house.

One of the pine trees we planted was small enough for me to jump over. When I visited the house with my wife almost forty years later, that tree had hardly grown. In an evil empire and its

---

13 Fenyo, Mario D., *Hitler, Horthy, and Hungary, German-Hungarian Relation, 1941—1944* (New Haven • London: Yale University Press, 1972).

satellites, I thought, hardly anything grows nor goes well. In a totalitarian regime with evil around, there is no blessing.

By the time Christmas came, people climbed into yards and sawed off the tops of trees, just to have Christmas trees. One of my father's friends had some money stolen. Years later, an apologetic letter arrived with the money, saying it had been needed for a Christmas present for the thief's family.

Still, my mother, being the cultural person in the family, took me to the opera, where I would see lovely girls my age with their mothers. In Europe, part of a good education is knowing who wrote an opera and what it is about. The opera of Budapest held a very high standard. Famous singers were often "booed-out" when they had succeeded in other capitals.

Toward the end of the war, I enjoyed German musicals which had sweet-sounding songs by talented composers. My film heroes at that time were Mickey Rooney and Judy Garland. I saw every movie of the "Andy Hardy" series and fell in love with all the actresses, just like Mickey Rooney did. I was one of those romantic boys who fell in love with love. I also remember seeing a well-produced German film on the sinking of the Titanic.

By the summer of 1944, German authorities no longer allowed anyone to leave German-occupied territories. Gone were Switzerland and Italy for vacation spots. But the road was open to the occupied territories, so along with many Hungarians we went to the Carpathian Mountains, which form a half-circle and engulf Czechoslovakia, Poland, and Romania. Unlike the Alps with their glaciers and meadows, the Carpathians are like the Rocky Mountains, full of beautiful pine forests, peaks, and cliffs.

Hungary had been included in the Carpathian circle when Slovakia belonged to her, but not when it was taken away through the Treaty of Versailles. However, part of Slovakia, once again, became a part of Hungary through the first Vienna Awards of 1938. More Hungarian leaders were seen in the hotels than Czech leaders. Actually, not much had really changed since 1919. The Hungarians had been there all along, and the Czechs never liked it.

Chechoslovakia was an industrial country with democratic

overtones between the two world wars. Her territories consisted of Bohemia, Moravia, Slovakia, and a small stretch on its eastern end, Ruthenia. These four powers guaranteed the territorial integrity of the country, but no one did anything when Hitler announced the annexation of Bohemia and Moravia on March 15, 1939, making it a protectorate.[14] Most of Slovakia became a nominally independent state, while the Hungarian kingdom got back the rest of Slovakia and Ruthenia.

Slovakia had several puppet leaders, like Monsenior Tiso who did everything Hitler commanded him to do. This short priest passed anti-Jewish legislation and was closely implemented with Germany in many other things. He was hanged after the war.

Heydrich became the Reich's protector of Bohemia and Moravia. A Nazi brute, he was involved in the "final solution of the Jews." Czech Nationals killed him during the war. Still, his widow could not understand why the people had not liked him.

Long before Hitler came to power, we often went to the "Tatra," an area in the Carpathian Mountains. The distance from Budapest was about seven hundred miles. You could go by train or private car. We would arrive at a mountain station called Poprad. From there, a small train would take us to the Tatra Mountains. There were fine hotels. One time I saw an attractive girl in the dining room of our hotel. I think she was the manager's daughter and I wanted to dance with her. Being fourteen and shy, I could not get up the courage to ask her, so my father did it for me and I got my wish.

In the summer, you could rest in the forests by mountain creeks, listening to the soft sound of the water disappearing among the pines. There were so many flowers, especially white, pink, and red phlox. They are still my favorite flowers and when I see them, I think of my youth and the Tatra.

I remember being there one Christmas with my parents and nanny, which I had until I was nine, and writing a letter in Ger-

---

14 Shoemaker, M. Wesley, *Russia, Eurasian States, and Eastern Europe* (Washington, D.C.: Stryker-Post Publications, 1996).

man to Kris Kringle. My nanny was a young woman from Germany, who died from tuberculosis after leaving us.

When we were in the Tatra Mountains in the summer of 1944, one could see and sense the German occupation everywhere. German officers and soldiers were in the hotels, and the Hitler Youth would march and sing at five o'clock in the morning, disturbing the guests. This was the last summer we went anywhere. After this, the Iron Curtain would descend on Eastern Europe, and for almost fifty years, Hungary would be like a prison.

The critical year of 1944 marks a black spot in Hungary's thousand-year history. The transformation would be so great that its consequences will be seen and discussed for a long time to come. The year's events changed Hungary's whole social structure, from aristocratic rule to one of the proletarian and working class, some leaders of which could hardly read.

When the Russians would occupy Hungary, they would demand war reparations for the next twenty years, yet they were no help in the rebuilding, financially or otherwise. They would even expect Hungary to take care of the occupying military forces. Hungary's coat of arms would be replaced with the Communist hammer and sickle, the hammer standing for the working class and the sickle standing for the peasantry.

Hungarian and German officials had met in Budapest on April 4, 1944, two weeks after Germany's occupation of Hungary, to carry out the "final solution of the Jews" in Hungary. On April 5, the Jews had to display the Star of David on their clothing. I saw them wearing it on the streets, streetcars, and buses. If one was caught without it, he did not live long.

By early summer, Eichmann, the German in charge of transporting all European Jews to the concentration camps, arrived in Budapest. The Hungarian Jews would be the last Jews to be shipped to their death. One of my classmate's father was supposed to stay and hide in a cellar. He did not and he never returned. His wife went to a death camp but she survived and came back.

To carry out his orders, Eichmann used cattle cars, which

were not easy to come by since the Germans had seized most of the livestock, grain, and machinery, taking them out of the country. At first, the Germans negotiated with the Hungarians for their goods, but nothing had ever come of those talks.

Often on nights when everything was quiet, we could hear shots in the distance. The Hungarian Nazis, called the Arrow Cross, either killed the Jews on the streets or marched them to the Danube, where they tied them up and threw them into the river. The Arrow Cross, also called the Green Shirts because of the color they wore, were cruel and shameless thugs, only sixteen or seventeen years old. This group tried to outdo even the German Nazis, who wore black and, along with the Romanian Iron Guard, were considered the most ruthless in Europe.

The various European countries reacted differently to the German onslaught. They either gave in, gave up, or continued to fight with armed or underground resistance, or sometimes just not cooperating. As Hitler swept across Europe, most countries gave in right from the beginning, Hungary being one of them. Even the Germans themselves were surprised.

Vesenmayer, the German plenipotentiary[15] in Budapest, testified at the Nuremberg trials that if Hungary had refused the German demands regarding the deportation of the Jews, there would have been nothing the Germans could have done on their own. Eichmann had only a small staff when Horthy finally stopped the deportations. The Germans were never in the position again to resume them.

France fought for a few days, but when the Germans breached the Maginot Line that the French thought was impregnable, Henry Petain made peace with the enemy. He had been the hero of Verdun, the fiercest battle of World War I. There is no sense to fight on, he thought. So he became a traitor, the head of the quasi-free Vichy Government, named for a health spa in Southern France. He constantly played into the hands of the Germans Because of him, thousands of children and adults

---

15 A diplomatic agent, such as an ambassador, fully authorized to represent his or her government.

were shipped to and perished in extermination camps.

General Charles de Gaulle wanted to continue the struggle, but in the end escaped to London with only his life. After the war, he put Petain, who was then in his nineties, on trial. The old man couldn't concentrate, only looking at the ladies' legs in the courtroom, so was saved from death and sent to a fort.

Some citizens gave up one another, along with Jews, to the Germans as if in a competitive race. In Holland, for instance, Anne Frank was discovered and betrayed by one of her father's employees, after she had hidden for several years. In Latvia and Estonia, cooperation with the Germans was commonplace and constant.

The finest example of "noncooperation" was in Denmark when the Germans' order came for the Jews to wear the Star of David. The Danish king came on the radio and said he would wear the star and expected all of his subjects to do the same. The Germans could not do anything

Russia chose to fight on, moving its armies from Siberia to Berlin, a stretch of seven thousand miles, an incomprehensible distance in those days to transport whole armies.

Although active in some countries more than others, the resistance movement prevailed. Germany itself had an underground, which tried to assassinate Hitler. However, it never succeeded. The last attempt was on July 29, 1944, when Count Stauffenberg planted a bomb at the "Woflschanze" (Wolf's lair), the headquarters in Prussia. The briefcase holding the bomb was moved and the bomb just slightly injured the "Ogre," the dictator.

There was also a Munich University student uprising, code-named "The White Rose." The students were printing anti-Nazi literature, but a janitor found it and turned them into the Nazis. After a mock trial, they were all executed.

France had the greatest underground resistance, called the "Maquis," a word stemming from the island of Corsica, where Napoleon was born. The inhabitants of this island constantly fought with each other, so they hid in the underbrush, the "maquis." The French underground was well organized and worked closely with the Allies to coordinate the invasion of Normandy. Its main leader was Georges Bidault, who in the end was arrested, tortured, and executed.

Hungary was not without its heroes. A Swede named Wallenberg came to Hungary and saved thousands of Jews with his skill and bluffing. He built Swedish houses, called "safe houses," through which Jews could move with passes that he copied by the thousands. Dealing with Eichmann, he was both fearless and relentless.

When Russia occupied Eastern Hungary and established a Communist government in Debrecen, Wallenberg wanted to reach them and negotiate the rebuilding of Budapest, and a favorable peace. But on the road, he disappeared, never to be seen or heard from again. People in the different camps of the "gulag," the Russian concentration camps in Siberia, would say they had seen him, but they were never sure.

Later, Mikhail Gorbachev announced that he had died a long time ago in a Moscow prison. There is a big statue of him in Budapest, and writings about him are quite extensive. President Reagan even made him an honorary citizen of the United States.[16]

---

16 Gorbachev was the president of the Soviet Union, and Reagan of the United States, during the 1980's.

The Powers That Be. . .

— the end of an era

In one of his classic short stories, the German writer, Henry Boll, tells about a young boy just out of high school, who comes home from the Eastern Front without his arms, but does not yet know this. He is wheeled into the classroom where he realizes that the writing on the blackboard is his very own, that it had not been erased. He tries to lean up with his elbows but falls back, realizing what the cruel war had done not only to him, but to millions of others. . .

As the Eastern Front moved closer to the Carpathian Mountains, the Germans needed to build airstrips. It was decided that high school students would do this work, and my gym teacher chose me, among others, to go to Karcag, an eastern town on the "puszta," or the plain. Some of our former teachers came with us, to serve by looking after us.

A school building was requisitioned, like so many times in war, in that dusty eastern town. Acacia trees, found in any Eastern European country as well as the Middle East, lined the streets. They are small with pink and white blossoms, giving off a fantastic sweet odor. I slept in that old school building in a classroom, on straw sacks. They would get full of fleas, smell after a while, and become flat from my weight. I remember a very black blackboard.

We were fed from the field kitchen, eating everything from one tin plate with one tin spoon. I had never been in a labor camp before, doing physical hard labor. So when I got out to the runway building site, I decided right then and there that I would not stay for long.

On the third or fourth day I somehow hurt my foot. I went

to the camp doctor, and he excused me from work. I had to stay, but as far I remember, I never had a shovel in my hands again.

Our teachers told us that after a while, we could go home on weekend passes. But that was not easy when Budapest was five hundred miles away, and the trains no longer kept to a schedule. They were used for military transportation, lines of cars with soldiers on them, or cannons, tanks, and trucks coming and going to and from the front. I did, however, get to visit home often during that summer and early fall of 1944. My mother always had the most delicious and pretty fruit trays prepared for me.

The Hungarian puszta is a fertile plain. It stretches from Budapest almost to the Russian border. It differs from the American prairie or the Russian steppes. It is hot and often the traveler sees mirages. The Hungarian cowboy is called a "csardas" if he herds cattle, and "gulyas" if horses. He has a beautiful, elaborate long leather coat that he carries halfway around his shoulders, using it at night when it gets cold.

Farms are called "tanyas" and are ten to twenty miles from each other. The wheat that grows on them produces the finest flour. It is quiet on the puszta, very quiet and lonely. Once, I slept on a big tall haystack. The night's blue sky twinkled with stars. The open space made me feel free. I also remember wells that looked like storks, their beaks holding the buckets that go down into the fresh water.

Once, I stood on a farm near a well. Out of the house came a young Gypsy girl. There were many gypsies in the Hungarian countryside, just as there were in other Eastern European countries. They lived in cornfields or wagons. The cornfields were so tall and vast that one could get lost in them. One of my classmates escaped from a concentration camp through cornfields. They never found him, and he even visited me after the war.

The gypsies were gifted in music, playing the violin from an early age. Little boys would board the trains, play their violins, get money thrown at them, and then get off at the next station. Gypsies were nomads, wandering around. They did not stay long in one spot. The different governments tolerated them, although they did not quite know what to do with them. Once, I saw a Gypsy being kicked and beaten. I tried to help, because I considered him a human being like myself.

According to Hitler, the Gypsies were trash and had to be gassed. The Nazi camp leaders made the Gypsy bands play before the gas chambers. One by one they were gassed and one by one the music stopped until there was just one left, then he also perished.[17]

There was a concentration camp for Jews not far from us, and once, another boy said to me that someone in the camp had told him I looked Jewish. I knew that I could easily end up in a death camp because I often read that half-Jews did, which I was since my mother was Jewish. God's hand was upon me again. I just did not know it at the time.

Every evening when dark descended, we would hear a plane overhead. It was the "Tito" bus, as we called it. It carried ammunition by the British to Josip Broz Tito, who was then the leader of the Yugoslavs against the Germans and the Croats. The Germans were often at Tito's heels, and he and his partisans were usually outdoors in either the summer heat or the winter cold. Later, Tito would become the president of Yugoslavia, meaning the "Southern Slavs." Yugoslavia was then comprised of seven provinces.

Off and on, I would talk in the labor camp with my German teacher, the one who had not been able to give me good grades. He wanted to know my opinion about the political situation. Then one evening in September, he surprised us by coming into the classroom and telling us that the Russians had broken through the passes of the Carpathian Mountains. Everyone was suddenly on his own to get home the best way he could.

I thought it would be interesting to go to Debrecen, a city I had never seen, farther east than we were and close to the Russian border. After which I would swing home. When I went to the station, the stationmaster did not know when the next train to Debrecen would be. Sometime the next day, he told me. The

---

17 Rarnati, Alexander, *And the Violins Stopped Playing, a Story of the Gypsy Holocaust* (New York: Franklin Watts, 1986).

trains could be as late as twenty-four hours, as they were used for military transport during the day and passengers at night.

It was already ten o'clock p.m., so I sat down by one of the tracks and waited, and waited. The air was chilly, as it is September. Within an hour or two, on another track, a hospital train pulled in. It stood there for quite a while, nurses getting off and on. I could see soldiers lying on bunks. I was pretty tired by then and thought how nice it would be to climb onto that train and rest for a while. Later, it pulled away in the dark, into the blackout.

The next day, I found myself in Debrecen. There was a famous theological seminary there, Debrecan being the bulwark of Hungarian Protestantism, or Calvinism. About thirty percent or more of Hungary is Protestant. I myself was raised a Presbyterian. The area Transdanubia, west of Budapest towards Austria, is Catholic. We did not change denominations in Hungary as easily as people do in the United States now.

I do not remember much of what I did that day, but towards evening, I went to the seminary and asked if I could spend the night. There were two students talking with each other when I fell asleep. As I woke up in the morning, they told me that I had slept through a long air raid. Obviously, I had been worn out from my long wait for the train, and my day in the city.

From Debrecen, it took me two days to get home. The trains were of course behind, their schedules having been thrown to the wind. On the journey, there was an air raid, and we passengers had to evacuate the train and go into the fields. We saw the bombs explode and fires, stirred by the wind, in the village ahead. My mother, again, had prepared a lovely fruit bowl for me.

I must have been home for only a few days when an order came for my class's conscription into the army, for the Western Front. My mother, understandably, was very upset. Her only son, eighteen years old, was going off to war. She packed my bag. I do not remember its contents. I walked to the city hall, where a long line of young men were already standing. Some I knew; some I did not. We were to be shipped out within an hour. I imagined my poor mother crying at home.

All at once, my father appeared. He somehow always commanded respect. He said to me, "Son, you will not go," and with that, he disappeared behind a door, into the office of the military doctor. Minutes passed. The door opened and my father came out with a slip of paper excusing me from the army. We went home, but I never knew what was written on that piece of paper. Neither do I know what he said to the doctor, maybe that I had a weak lung, which was true. In any case, I recognized later how Almighty God was still directing and planning my life.

October 15,1944, dawned a chilly autumn day. The population did not realize what a fateful day this would become for all of Hungary. My parents and I stepped out on our balcony that overlooked a great part of Buda, including the royal palace in its neo-Baroque style, and the Matthias Cathedral where many kings had been crowned. Within six weeks, this would become the frontline in a theater of war, and completely destroyed.

We can hear a soft humming. It is the steady traffic of the city. The trees still have their leaves. Before us is an empty yard. Behind us, within four months, we will bury eight German soldiers who will lose their lives in the onslaught on our house, and in the cause of a hopeless war. We would take their dog tags and send them back to Germany. To my knowledge, their remains still lie there, behind our house in that cold ground.

We have heard rumors that something big is going to happen. There was a proclamation earlier on the radio from Regent Horthy: "Today it is clear to any sober thinking person that the German Reich has lost the war. I have the duty to undertake every step in order to prevent further bloodshed." When we heard this, we cheered Finally, Budapest would be saved. For us, we thought, the war was over.

> By five o'clock p.m. that day, everything was decided . . . Horthy was convinced . . .that all of Hungary was marching firmly behind him, but on that day he found out that even in his own closest circle, very few seriously took their oath of allegiance to him. Horthy's efforts on this day were slowly foiled by the Hungarian army

officers' corps. Senior officers issued in his name false proclamations contradicting the Regent, and subordinates arrested their commanding officers who remained loyal to Horthy. As for the population, it received the Regent's appeal with its usual . . . indifference and apathy, but in some cases with . . .hostility.[18]

After the proclamation, the whole country was delivered into the arms of the Arrow Cross, and a reign of terror began. The Arrow Cross's headquarters were at Andressy Street 60, which took up almost a block. Later, during the Soviet's rule, this building would house the Communist regime, and the street renamed People's Republic Street. When people on the street approached it, they would cross the street to avoid it. Thousands were tortured in the basement, without cause. In every country, Nazi-controlled or Communistic, there were headquarters for torturing. In Paris, for example, it was in the Rue Lauristan.

The Romanians, for whom Hungary had nothing but contempt, united under their young King Michael and so saved their country from turning into a battlefield. There were no informers or traitors, and the officer corps remained faithful to its oath to the king. As its reward, Romania "re-annexed" Transylvania. Hungary, on the other hand, was dangerously divided, its fate determined by its inability to make a decision, and its hesitation to do so. Once again, history repeated itself.

The Communists would change almost everything in Hungary that reminded them of the old regime. Not just the name of streets, but the monetary system as well. Once, my father had joked that if the Russians invaded our house, he would eat supper with them. He even saved Hungarian wine for such an occasion. I idolized my father and he was right most of the time, but not then. He, like the rest of Europe and the world, did not yet know the "Red Army" and its brutality.

---

18 Nagy-Talaver, Nicholas M., *The Green Shirts and the Others, a History of Facism in Hungary and Rumania* (Stanford, California: Hoover Institution Press, 1970).

A Thief in the Night. . .

— the siege of Budapest

I remember the almost indescribable feeling of being a civilian in a city surrounded by enemy troops, and knowing that your life and your family's lives were at stake. I felt helpless, so much had suddenly changed, so much was yet to change and never be the same. Budapest would nearly be destroyed as much as Stalingrad, where in the end, they fought not just for ruined buildings, but for plain stones. Or like Warsaw where the Germans destroyed not just the city itself, but the blueprints so it could never be restored. My memory of that time can never be erased, nor should it be, as its horror and my survival helped me know that God definitely was in charge of my life . . .[19] [20]

Within two weeks of overthrowing the government, the Arrow Cross was in our house. It was the afternoon and I was taking a piano lesson. The doorbell rang outside in the garden and I opened the gate. I hurried back to the house and there they stood, some Green Shirts. They forced themselves into the house, demanding I wake my father who was taking his nap. He had done so from three to four o'clock every day, and had yet to deviate from it.

They ordered us into the living room to sit and not move. One aimed his gun at us and said that he had just killed seven Jews before coming to our house. My piano teacher was quite upset because her husband was a Socialist deputy, but they let

---

19 To my knowledge, there is not much writing on the Siege of Budapest. One story, *I Am Fifteen and I Don't Want to Die*, by Christine Arnothy, was published in 1956 and became a bestseller in Paris

20 Arnothy, Christine. *I Am Fifteen and I Don't Want to Die* (New York: An Eagle Book Popular Library, 1956).

her go later. Those thugs began searching our house, looking for Communist literature, they said. Later on, my father discovered they had stolen his Patek watch from his nightstand. This kind of Swiss watch, of which only one thousand are made every year, was 22 karat gold. One of these watches can be worth from three thousand to four thousand dollars, depending on how old it is, if it is a pocket watch, or if it has chimes.

After the war, my father gave two of his gold pocket watches to a gentleman leaving for Vienna, asking him to deliver them to my uncle, one of my mother's brothers. When I left Budapest and stayed with my uncle after the Hungarian Revolution in 1956, he gave me those watches as I left for the United States. Those two watches are the only things I have of my inheritance, along with the baby book my mother kept of me until I was six years old. I have kept those watches in a bank vault for forty years.

After the Arrow Cross went through almost everything, they wanted to see our papers, to see if we were Jewish. They had found some newspaper clippings about Jews and asked why we had kept them. My father was borderline diabetic and had a supply of saccharin. They asked him why he had so much because during the war, hoarding was forbidden, punishable by a five or six-year prison sentence.

Their search lasted for about three hours, but they found no Communist literature. Still, they told us, they could not leave without us and had to take us to headquarters. They took us to a big room on the fifth floor. I could hear them talking, calling each other "sister" and "brother." Then they brought in a gentleman whom my parents seemed to know, an old military officer from the old regime. I can still see him lying on the floor, curling up, and holding his foot. I don't know what was wrong with him, but I never saw him again. Then sirens started howling and everyone went to the basement except us. Later, though, they came back for us and took us down to safety. When my mother was cold and shivering, they brought her a blanket, proving they had some kindness left in them. We spent the whole night there, but in the morning they did not let us go back home.

Instead, they took us to a hotel and locked us up in a room.

The jails were full. Not with criminals, but with political prisoners. The Arrow Cross themselves were the criminals. I met twenty other people in that hotel room. My father and I were with the men. My poor mother was with the women. I always saw her looking out the door to catch a glimpse of her loved ones. Looking back now, I realize how much she was just beginning to suffer.

When they locked us in that hotel room, I made the acquaintance of men with high-ranking social status. They were parliamentarians, professors, and one was even a general. He always sat in the bathroom on the toilet seat. I assume that was the most comfortable place in the room. One professor told me he was there because he was Jewish, that one of his students had betrayed him to the Arrow Cross.

This professor instructed me on how to behave during interrogations and torture—not to be haughty, but polite and humble. The goal was to not make the Arrow Cross angry. The interrogations went on day and night. One morning a count was thrown back into the hotel room, beaten half to death.

Then my father and I were interrogated together. Just one man was there when we were led into a room. The man was polite and did not touch us. Once again, my father proved his respectability.

We saw and heard distant explosions as the Russians moved towards the capital. We would first see the fire, then hear the sound. Closer and closer the front came every day. I don't think the schools opened in the fall of 1944. It was already November and I would have been at the university by then. My father wanted me to attend Law school, but there would be other things to think about in the months ahead.

Without even straw sacks to sleep on, we put our heads on one another's legs. There was one particular gentleman who would snore loudly and then suddenly wake up. Apparently, he was suffering shell shock from World War I.

Then the policeman on duty came and called our names. We could leave. We walked up the hill and as we arrived home, we saw the gardener working in the yard, though the weather had turned cold. But our house had a boiler, which heated the whole house. Along with his yard work, the gardener kept the boiler fed with coal, a tremendous chore as the coal was stored in its own room.

We also had a laundry room, where the maid's only tools were a big tub and a large bar of soap. My room was right overhead and I remember noticing on laundry day steam rising past my window from below. For a few years, we were probably the only ones who had a refrigerator. It was small and made by Bosch, a German company. I always heard it humming as I fell asleep in my room.

We were at home for about two weeks when the doorbell rang. My mother opened the door and there stood a member of the Arrow Cross in front of her. She was frightened, but he told her he would not arrest us again, that the Arrow Cross only wanted to use our house for their party headquarters. For quite a while, nothing happened. Then one day, a young man came and told us that the "party" had sent him. We knew what he meant and let him in. We gave him my room and everything continued as it normally had. He seemed satisfied occupying just one room.

In a few days, a woman appeared with a young boy. She was supposed to be the man's wife. "The Russians are after us," she said as she introduced herself. She drove a Mercedes, probably taken from Jews. We had a Mercedes, also, but no longer used it ourselves. The army had use of it whenever they wanted. It would be the first thing the Russians would confiscate, with much more to come.

Christmas was approaching but there would be no celebration. There were no Christmas trees, and not many gifts because most of the stores were already closed. The frontline was on the outskirts of Budapest, and the Russians stood before the city gates.

I remember our Arrow Cross "resident" storming in on Christmas Eve, telling us that the Russians had broken through and were in the hills two miles behind our house. When we woke up the next day, Christmas day, his whole family was gone. We never knew how they left without making any noise, car and all. My dear mother met the woman after the siege of

Budapest. She told her she had no knowledge of her husband at that time. Who knows if she ever found him.

In two days, the Red Army surrounded our big city, so tightly that not even a mouse could escape. We lost our access to water, and gas for heat. One hundred thousand German and Hungarian troops were trapped. The Soviets sent two representatives to try and negotiate a settlement that would prevent a senseless siege of destruction. They were murdered. After that, Stalin gave the Soviet army a free hand, and the destruction of Budapest began.

Two days after Christmas, 1944, we were already so cold that we had to put on our fox fur coats. When I escaped Hungary during the revolution in 1956, I wore one and still have it to this day. That winter, my fingers would freeze. Still, when I touch something cold or icy, my fingers start to hurt and even burn.

Because there was no water, we could not wash our hands or faces, or bathe. We found a small iron stove and built a fire with some coal. More smoke came from that stove than heat, but we were still able to melt some snow on top of it and so wash up a little. All we had to eat were beans, beans, and more beans. Later on we ate the horses that had died on the roads. It was so cold that the meat stayed fresh. We would. carve ourselves chunks, take them home, and cook them on the stove. Horsemeat isn't bad, as it tastes sweet and makes a good Hungarian goulash.

We had flour for making bread but not the means to bake it, so I took the flour down three houses from us where a family had a big oven. One day, I found only half a house. The whole family gone. A shell had hit them and wiped out everybody. I walked slowly back up the hill and told my parents. Life is that frail, I thought. One moment we are here, the next we are gone. Isaiah said, "*All men are like grass, and all their glory is like the flowers of the field. . .The grass withers, and the flowers falls, but the word of our God shall stand forever.*" (Isa. 40:6-8 NIV) God's hand was again protecting me, but I did not know it then.

During the siege, we were told not to approach the windows, and when the fighting became rougher we moved down to the basement. It had a long hallway about nine feet wide with doors on both sides. We chose one dark, windowless room, where we put two boxes together, a plank across them, and a mattress on top covered with sheets. We did not know it yet, but our stay in the basement was to last several months. Compared to the German population that lived in basements for years like rats, and in blockhouses where strangers had to endure each other, our confinement was not so bad.

By then, all of our windows upstairs had been broken from the pressure of exploding bombs, so we had used plywood to nail shut the openings, leaving three-inch gaps at the tops. It made it darker, but kept the cold from streaming in full force. Every night we went to bed early, as did everybody else. There was nothing else to do and sleeping helped us forget the misery around us. Plus we couldn't feel our hunger when we slept. I remember my mother being unhappy that she was unable to feed me enough.

Sometimes at night, we would venture outside and walk around the house. It was quiet, without the usual activity, as even the troops had to eat and sleep. One night, I saw my father digging at the end of the yard. He was burying some of my mother's jewelry. After the war, when our villa had been taken over by the communist government, I tried to locate those buried jewels. But the shrubs and trees had grown and changed just enough that I couldn't find them. We had packed all of my parents' art, such as paintings, in carts and put them in the basement with us.

The shelling became continuous in the distance behind our house, where the front lay. A row of heavy artillery cannons were closer, covered with fine lace curtains from houses. The Russians hit the row of apartments in the valley below, one of which my father owned. It had been five stories with twenty-one apartments. Our villa was also hit several times but since the walls were two feet thick and the roof was extraordinarily strong, the damage was not too great. I remember a fifty-pound bomb boring itself into the side of our house, but not exploding. A German soldier put it on his shoulders and carried it out to the street.

Somewhere, in one of the empty lots by our house, I was sure there was a machine gun nest. During the day, I could hear it almost continuously, but I could never find where it was or who operated it. I just remember its constant racket— how unnerving and upsetting it was. Sometimes, we heard loudspeakers all night from the Pest side, across the Danube, shouting in Hungarian to stop the fighting, that the fighting was senseless and just led to more destruction.

On January 18, 1945, Pest fell. The beautiful bridges had been blown up by the retreating German garrison. The fighting had gone from house to house and block to block. There was not an inch of territory that the Russians had not touched, no ground on which they had not trod. Everything and everyone had been violated in one way or another. There had been rape, and even murder of civilians. Every building had Cyrillic (Russian) letters painted on the walls, probably directions for the troops.

After the siege, the Russians took tens of thousands of civilians as prisoners and put them in camps. They had told their leaders that they had taken more prisoners of war than they really had, so the civilians made up the difference. My best friend was one of those taken. We used to discuss movies and philosophy. By January 1945, however, he would be dead. He was put into a camp of ten thousand in the middle of winter, and typhoid broke out, not only killing him but many others.

He was also half-Jewish, if such a thing exists. He and his parents moved from the hills to downtown to be safer. They were not. He had visited me the last time in early December, before they moved. That was the last time I saw him alive. His father was notified about his death and at least was able to pick up his body. How difficult that must have been.

The Russians picked me up also, only every day, to dig ditches, and I came home every night. Why, I do not know. Once again, the providence of God.

My friend's father was president of a great company. After the Communist takeover, he wanted to import coolers from England, like ones found in grocery stores. They imprisoned him for contacting the West, which was a crime. My father asked me to take him some food and a blanket. As I waited in the prison, I heard screams, I assume, of someone being tortured.

By now it was toward the end of January. The fighting was all around us, and it was cold with much snow. For light, we used a can of gasoline and a string for a wick. I can still see the finger-thick smoke coming from it, and smell its stench. The light it gave off was at best two inches in diameter.

One day, as my father and I opened the door of one room and went in, a bullet shot through the slit in a window and exploded. One inch closer and it would have hit me. The bullets the Russians used not only penetrated but also blew up. Sharp shooters must have heard the door open and seen the slit in the window, otherwise they wouldn't have been shooting at us.

The sound of battle was constant, a mix of machine-gunning, shooting flares, and tanks moving around, along with explosions. This went on for weeks, constantly, and became hard to take, breaking our nerves.

On the last two nights in January, we again walked outside around the house. As we approached one side of the fence, we saw it had been cut, and there were three or four men in white camouflage. We asked them what they wanted. They told us to be quiet and we returned to the house. Within minutes, eight to nine Germans appeared in our basement. They had fled from the neighbors' houses, which the Russians had set on fire. The Russians were occupying the whole street except for our house, because it was the biggest and they knew the Germans would defend it.

The next day the German Commander, a tall handsome man, appeared with the soldiers. He told us how beautiful our house would be in peace time, and that he understood what it must be like for us, that his family had been bombed-out several times in Berlin. He then explained that he had orders to fight from house to house. He asked me to come upstairs with him to show him the layout of the rooms. As we approached a window, we heard shooting again.

The Germans pushed all the heavy furniture in front of the doors and windows, and threw all the keys away. But the

Russians would not need keys when they stormed our house. They would only need hand grenades. The commander suggested that we move into the main hallway because the walls were thick enough to withstand bullets and explosives. There we settled down to wait. Everything was quiet. Not a shot could be heard. We knew that the Russians were preparing for an attack against our house, an eerie feeling indeed.

To be trapped in a big city surrounded by enemy troops is one thing, but to be trapped in your own home is much worse. When it was quiet for two to three days, I asked a German to explain it. Just wait, he told me, it's the quiet before the storm. I wondered what would happen. If my father would wine and dine with the Russians as he had declared he would, or if we would be taken prisoner, or even murdered? We were to find out soon.

I felt sorry for myself. I should have been in Switzerland. My teenage years should have been filled with positive experiences, and there I was, instead, waiting for the "red hordes" to attack. My house felt like a tomb, with no way in and no way out. The Germans themselves knew there was no escape. The only escape route had been the day before, through the vineyard on the other estate behind ours. I could have left, the commander told me, but I didn't want to be separated from my parents. Plus I knew I would encounter more of the same elsewhere. There was no escape from Budapest, period.

The Germans were scared. They were constantly moving back and forth, and in and out of rooms. After all, the frontline was the street outside our entry gate. The Russians were squatting behind our red stone fence, a natural defense for them. Our house had three huge balconies facing the city, which the Germans used for their heavy machine guns. Most of the German soldiers stayed in the bunker with us, their commander remaining calm and brave.

We lost track of time. We had our watches but it was dark both day and night. Everyone knew something was going to happen any moment. During the night of February 1st, around three o'clock in the morning, things changed. Out of the quiet, the storm broke loose. The Germans on duty ran down to the basement and wakened the commander. He went upstairs and then back again, saying the Russians were preparing for an attack, that we should stay in the hallway downstairs. As he returned to the main floor, he called for his aid, Konig, but he was nowhere to be found.

The next moments brought complete silence. Then there was a big explosion when the first grenade was thrown against our house. Silence again. The machine guns started and made our big house tremble. We did not know what was going on. We just stood there in the hallway in the dark. Then came another explosion that bent an iron door leading from the boiler room to the hallway where we were. By now we were completely confused by the shooting machine guns, explosions, and mixture of voices, combined with darkness and smoke.

The Russians were shouting and we starting shouting, "Civilian, civilian!" The gardener's baby cried in his arms I saw red bullets whistling by our faces in the dark hallway, then out of the darkness and smoke and screaming emerged a Russian boy. He might have been seventeen years old. He could have killed us, but he suddenly stopped shooting. This was strange since a piece of bread was worth more than a human life in Budapest then.

The Russians, like lice, had poured through their breach in our home. They were all camouflaged in white. They lined us up and herded us into the boiler room. I instinctively scrunched my head into my shoulders as if protecting myself from bullets and shrapnel. My father, so calm in such a critical situation, asked me if I was afraid.

We were told not to touch the red flag on the roof, the sign that they occupied the house. This was necessary as the frontline zigzagged, occupying one house and not necessarily its neighbor. The situation would worsen when the Germans would reoccupy a house. It was hard enough to have one's house occupied once, but twice was almost too much to bear. Yet we had no choice.

It was snowing heavily outside as we sat in the boiler room. The Russians had drums in their machine guns, with sixty-five bullets each, different from the German and American designs. They would throw the empty drum away, and push in a full one. They pointed their guns out the windows, firing every so often.

A Russian came for the gardener. The Germans were supposedly upstairs, but because the Russians did not want to get shot, they did their dirty work with civilians. There were no Germans, but one Austrian was hiding among the furniture. They took him prisoner and paraded him in front of us before taking him away. I knew that the Russians did not treat their prisoners with gloved hands, but with cruelty, like the Japanese did to the Chinese and the Americans. I could only imagine what would happen to him.

Wolves in Sheep's Clothing. . .

— a premature celebration

Within forty-eight hours, the Hungarian and German aristocratic system would change completely to a Russian communistic one, as quickly as the frontline had changed. . .

As that first day of fighting wore on, the Russians continued to direct their guns out the basement windows. When the Germans escaped by jumping from the balconies, they literally landed in the line of fire. All were massacred, except the commander, who was not among them. He was the last to leave the basement, so must have seen what was going on. I do not know what happened to him, but he was not among the bodies we buried a few days later behind our house. The Red Army took care of its own dead.

By evening, the Russians who had first occupied our home were gone. But that was just the first wave, whose job it was to fight, capture, and go on to the next house. Other Russians would replace them. This second wave would stay a few more days or weeks, although its objective was still military in nature. However, it did begin to direct and control every aspect of our lives. The third wave, called the occupying force, would restore civil order. In other words, the fighting would stop.

When night came, nobody really slept. Those moments when I did doze off, I had nightmares about the bodies in the yard I had seen earlier in the day. Dozens of Russians swarmed around in the hallway and the dark room where we had our cot. Polish partisans, who were fighting with them, also joined us in our bunker. I remember one Russian standing in the doorway all night, scraping his back against the wall. I assume he had lice, for the fighting troops had no chance to wash for days on end. They also smoked, what I don't know, but it filled up our room with a horrible stench.

In the morning, after a heavy barrage that the Russians had to wait out before they could continue fighting, an officer told me and our gardener to leave the house and go up the hill for identification purposes. They considered this necessary to keep the male population from congregating and possibly revolting. My mother started crying and an older Russian assured her that I would come back.

As we stepped into the open air, I looked around and virtually did not recognize the landscape. I had lived in those hills for many years, but now the telephone lines were down, the roads were littered, and snow covered everything. A frontline scene in the dead of winter. I can no longer recall what road the Russians took us on to their "commandaturou," their headquarters, about two miles farther up into the hills. But I do remember everyone being interrogated, whether they were "Nazi sympathizers" or not.

Our gardener, who came with me, was questioned first. Although he was behind closed doors, I will never forget the beautiful words I overheard. He told them what fine people we were and that we were far from being Nazi sympathizers. At that time, when so many people were being smeared by witnesses, false or otherwise, and being dragged through the streets of Europe, our gardener's testimony was unique. Eventually, everyone would go through "de-Nazification" courts all over Europe, in which witnesses would either vouch for a person's guilt or innocence.

My interrogation did not last long and we were free to go back home, but that was not easy with the fighting in the streets. The frontline was still a zigzag, with some homes occupied by Germans and others by Russians, the new masters. They told us to wait until nightfall but we decided to try it anyway.

Those two miles took the rest of the day. We could have easily been picked up by sharpshooters. When we finally arrived at our house in the dark, there were patrols who would not let us in. Naturally, they could not have known that we lived there. Finally, we convinced them somehow, and my mother was so happy to have her son again.

As the occupation continued, Russian soldiers were looting, raping, and murdering, although their commanders had told them not to. I remember standing with an eighteen-year-old girl in our basement when a Russian soldier came and took her into another room. I wasn't stupid—I knew what was happening. Down the hill from us lived a wealthy family with a teenage daughter. The Russians wanted to rape her, but the father stepped in to protect her. His reward was the Russians killing all of them.

Hiding was impossible, as the Russians were everywhere, but a young girl could be spared rape if she made herself look older and not as pretty. Usually a scarf around her head did the job, and the addition of a baby proved to be even more of a deterrent. The Russians loved babies. "Matuschka, matuschka," they would cry out and go on, not molesting the girl.

Meanwhile, the looting by the civilian population went on. We were not allowed upstairs. I would listen at night to the constant tramping upstairs. There must have been hundreds of people coming and going as the front moved on. Later, when we finally went upstairs, we met utter devastation. Things were hacked to pieces. My father's library books were on the floor and torn apart. We found charred coal in the middle of one room where the Russians must have made a fire. Ninety-five percent of our rubbing alcohol had disappeared, for the Russians had drunk it as if it were vodka.

With the maid and cook gone, my mother cleaned up most of the mess. She was able to save some family pictures from the trash, some of which I have today. They still show the marks of dirt and mud. They remind me of what she must have gone through, of how the war must have contributed to her early death at the age of fifty-nine.

Every night, the Russians would come with flashlights, shining them in our faces. They would make us get up and go to work outside. In the middle of the night, in the snow, we had to carry bombs and push cannons. It did not matter to them that we went without sleep. One time, three Russian soldiers appeared in our basement. They pointed at my parents and me, ordering us to take our coats and go out to the yard. There they would shoot us, they said. Everyone froze from fear, then slowly followed them outside. Out of nowhere, a Russian officer appeared. The soldiers, who were drunk, suddenly scattered. Again, God's timing saved me. One-half minute later, and we all would have been dead.

As I mentioned earlier, the Russians would use civilians for dangerous jobs. Our lives were not worth a penny. They told my father to go down the road to see if there were any Germans. He started walking and noticed German soldiers standing patrol at the corner. He could not turn back and run, for that would have looked suspicious. So he continued to walk slowly. The Germans asked him where he was going. To the drug store, he answered, the first thing that came to his mind, and he walked on. For a few seconds, nothing happened, then the Germans shouted that there was no drug store and started shooting. By then, my father must have been out of their range. He detoured around them and returned home safely.

By February 12, 1945, the siege was over. The sound of battle had quieted down. The remaining German garrison had dug itself into the underground tunnels of the Royal Palace and surrounding area. The Turks had built them four hundred years earlier.

That evening, the Russians told me to come outside to give them directions. I will never forget the scene. On a country road not too far away, I saw hundreds of vehicles, tanks, and cannons, and thousands of Russians milling around in the snow. The cannons that had previously bombarded the apartments below were now turned around and lined up in case of a German assault. I never gave any directions. I don't know why, as the Russians could have shipped me to Siberia. Instead, I went back home.

As the days went on, people stopped at our house looking for family members. They had been separated from each other during the bombings and various evacuations. One day we heard that some Schutzstaffel (SS) men had sneaked into our area. SS men were easily recognized because of a tattoo on their left arm. The Russians would catch them and execute them on the spot.

This happened in the wake of Hitler's commissar order, which said that any Russian commissar caught on the Russian front was to be shot by the German army. The commissars were political indoctrinators, holding political rallies and teaching Marxism. They would follow the soldiers and shoot them for cowardice.

A few weeks after the Russians began their occupation of Hungary, all the male population had to dig a continuous ditch around Budapest, in ten degrees below zero. With shovels and picks, we worked eight to ten hours a day on that frozen ground.

When we went home at night, Russian patrols would catch people and put them back to work. Our telling them that we had just come from work, that we were tired and wanted to go home, did not make any difference. They could not understand us. So we avoided them, telling each other which routes to take to get around them.

My parents had friends who received a postcard from their son, who was on his way home from Siberian captivity. But he ran into a Russian patrol five blocks from his home, and they shipped him back to Siberia for years. I was so fortunate to always get home safely. God must have had his hand on me then. I know He did.

As the weeks went by, we ventured down from the hill. There was not a building that had not been destroyed. Rubble was piled three stories high. We had to walk everywhere, because no means of transportation had yet been restored. As it became warmer, the hundreds, perhaps thousands of bodies in the rubble began emitting an immense rotting stench. The rubble, the stench, remained for months.

The Russians wanted me to work in the neighborhood cleaning horses. An actress owned a ranch-style house down the hill from us. I remember the Russians kicking her in the behind and telling her that from now on, she would live in her maid's room. About thirty horses were tied down at the windowsills in the rest of the rooms. The Russians gave me a brush and a bucket of water, and every morning for several hours, I would clean those horses that the Russian officers then rode, showing off. After all, we were the vanquished— they were the masters.

The Russians kept a wagon full of bread in the yard. Every time I left for home, I stole a loaf. That's how hungry we were. One time, an older Russian caught me and I started running. I expected him to catch up with me, but he never did. The next day, all the Russians, and their bread, were gone.

On May 7, 1945, peace came to Europe. At least the frontlines fell silent. Many were still to lose their lives through land mines and such. I myself did not know what peace was. I did not know what neon-lit streets or stores were because I had grown up with war and blackouts. I had gotten so accustomed to this way of life. Men came home from the war with beards. Nowadays, if I see a man with a beard, I think of the postwar period, that a beard is unnatural in peacetime.

Times continued to be hard even after the end of the war. Rationing of food and fuel went on and on. Only babies got milk. We did not know about vitamins, and I did not see oranges or bananas for many years. We ate meat only twice a week and everything was expensive, as inflation had lifted its ugly head. It drove everyone crazy to have to carry money in suitcases and count it out in the billions. Money that had some value in the morning was worthless by the evening. Then came devaluation. The government declared that one million would now be one "florint" in the new monetary system.

Then there was the housing problem. Many people had been bombed-out and needed to stay somewhere. The city management made a list of houses and rooms and randomly sent people to live there. We ended up living in just two rooms of our house. Strangers, couples or single people, took up the rest of the rooms. We shared the kitchen and the bathroom with them, a hard change from our previous life.

This situation led to "infighting" among the house residents. Understandably, you wanted to have your own relatives or friends live with you. So you went to an influential person in the housing department and asked him, or even bribed him, to evict the strangers and replace them with people you knew. My father paid in paintings, one of the ways he lost his wealth. All in vain, as it turned out. Our housing situation did not change.

Our five-story apartment building was in rubble, so my father found an architect to rebuild it. After completion, they each would have owned half. But the day the project was completed, the government confiscated it. In other words, it was nationalized. By 1951, the government would nationalize all houses and apartment buildings over six rooms. Neither could factories, firms, or cars be owned by citizens.

I remember a man coming to see my father the day the government seized practically everything. He told my father that he no longer owned our villa on the hill. We had to pay rent for our own home. This wiped out our whole fortune. Besides a few paintings, my father had nothing left. Everything had been taken from him. He could not find his place in this strange new communistic world. Then, I did not understand, but now, looking back, I feel so very sorry for him.

After the war was over, millions of children were orphaned and abandoned on the streets, not knowing what to do or what line of thought to embrace. Many adults found themselves in the same dilemma. They had all lived with Nazism alone. Whole families committed suicide by shooting themselves or taking poison. They could not fathom another world, another system other than the Nazi one. Gobbels, the Nazi propaganda minister, and his actress wife, had five daughters whom they killed with poison, along with themselves. That's how much they had believed their own propaganda. Nothing else made sense. Like the orphans felt after the war, there was just nothing left.

Countries, as well as individuals, had to struggle with their past crimes. Hans Frank, the Governor General of Poland, said before his execution, "A thousand years will pass, and the crimes Germany committed will not be erased." Germany is still haunted by the Jewish question, as is Russia. The people of Israel are God's chosen, and anyone touching them touches the "apple of His eye." Those who do are bound to suffer and pay, in some way.

The Truth Shall
Make You Free. . .

— a change of heart

Dance fever had taken over Europe after the war, and big band tunes resounded everywhere. I was romantically inclined as a boy, falling in love with this circus performer or that actress. Mostly, I was in love with love. So the sweet tunes of Gershwin, Cole Porter, and Glenn Miller became "my songs." I mainly dated one girl, a lawyer's daughter. Later, she went to Switzerland to work for the Red Cross. During the Hungarian Revolution of 1956, when I would escape to Vienna, I heard she was there working on behalf of the Hungarian Refugee Relief. I visited her briefly in her hotel, but never saw her again. She probably thought we would get married, but I would instead leave for America. . .

My mother had not been well for quite a while. She tired easily and felt poorly. Her energy was gone and she could no longer do everything she had for us. Many times, she tried to hide her weakened condition from us. At first, I didn't notice. I was too busy with parties and dances.

Then my mother had to go to the hospital, actually a makeshift sanitarium run by Catholic nuns. She had a very high fever, so they gave her dosage after dosage of penicillin, the only antibiotic at that time. My father and I visited her, but she did not improve. One night, my father was deep in thought. "Son," he told me. "Your mother is very, very sick." I became uneasy and restless. Even with the war around me, I had never thought about my mother dying. I was, after all, only twenty years old. My mind started racing. I thought about all the times I had been disrespectful to her, how I had disobeyed her, how harsh I had been with her.

Something was very wrong with me. I wanted to find the solution, but I did not know how or where to find one. I just knew somehow that God was angry or disappointed with me. If I could just ask my mother for forgiveness, then all would be right. So one evening, I let my father go on home without me. I sat down at my mother's bedside. She looked away towards the wall, so I would not see how very sick she was, as it turned out, with leukemia.

I gathered my courage to ask her, "Mother, can you forgive me for all the times I was disrespectful to you?"

My mother turned to me and replied, "Of course, a mother can forgive her son." With that answer, I ran after my father. It was the last time I saw my mother alive. She died during the night, on October 1, 1946.

When my mother's funeral was over, we went home. It was so very quiet and lonesome. Our Presbyterian minister told me later that my father had visited him and cried. That was natural, I suppose. My parents had loved each other, but he didn't want me to see his tears.

Since my mother had forgiven me, I thought my torment would be over and I would experience peace. But I did not. I still had to settle things with God. Then a schoolmate visited me. He told me about a summer camp he had gone to and how there, he had met Christ. I had never heard that someone could "meet" Christ. I went to church because my parents sent me, but mostly I wanted to either see a friend or show off a new suit.

My schoolmate invited me to a Bible study for young people. Again, I had never been at a Bible study, nor had I read the Bible. I really didn't understand it. So at first, I was not serious about going. Later, I would make it a point to be there. When I entered the room, I could not believe my eyes. Everyone was my age, so I felt comfortable right away. Then they started praying, asking and thanking the Lord for being there with them. I had often prayed before falling asleep, but my words had just gone to the ceiling, and no farther. My heart had not been in them.

That evening, after my first Bible study, I went home and

dug out my Bible. I started reading it. Slowly the words began to have meaning, reality. And I felt they were directed to me. I sensed that God loved me and was seeking my love in return. I began to realize that His love for me was both personal and everlasting. Jeremiah 31:3 (NIV) says, *"I have loved you with an everlasting love; I have drawn you with loving- kindness."*

One night I was sitting at my mother's desk and reading the Scriptures. I came to a verse in John 6:37 (King James): *"All that the Father giveth me shall come to me; and him that cometh to me I will no wise cast out."* Suddenly it hit me. Did this mean that if I came to Jesus, he would not cast me out? Even with all of my flaws and sins? As I reread this verse, I told God that I could not solve my problems by myself. I told him that if he would accept me, I would give my life to Christ and let Him into my heart.

The result was a renewed life. My whole outlook changed and my problems faded away—my sins were forgiven because Christ had died on the cross for them. His blood washed them away forever. What a relief. I decided to serve God from then on, in whatever I did, in whatever profession He led me. I made a commitment to Him, but considered this easy after all He had done for me, after protecting me so many times, and after promising me so much.

I had been afraid of death, but God now assured me of my salvation. In John 3:16 (NIV), He says, *"Whoever believes in Him shall not perish but have eternal life."* The word *"have"* is in the present tense—not in the distant future. At the moment we believe, we have eternal life and nobody can take it from us. The Holy Spirit puts a seal on it. *"And I give them eternal life,"* John 10:28 (NIV) says, *"and they shall never perish; no one can snatch them out of my hand."*

When the Red Army invaded Hungary, through postwar agreements with the other Allies, it was given a free hand. They not only militarily devastated the countryside and cities in Eastern Europe, but forced their ideology on those they conquered. They left God out of their belief system, and in so doing were in darkness and had a distorted picture of life. Only with God can people know reality and ultimate truth. Christ says, *"I am the way and the truth and the life."* (John 14:6 NIV)

Although Russia had occupied Hungary quickly, its complete takeover was gradual. From 1947 to 1950, the government still consisted of a multi-party system. Even the churches had freedom to continue their worship services and other activities. Outside established religion, a great revival took place in Hungary those same three years. Bible studies spread throughout the country, their members ultimately filling the churches. Young people began to confront their pastors, asking them if they knew Christ, if they were "born again." Students in seminaries did likewise with their professors.

Though this national revival was not led or organized by churches, it began with the Presbyterian Christian Endeavor (CE) Youth Movement, which had been prevalent in the United States during the 1930's. It had its own campground not far from Budapest, and its leaders proved to be spiritual giants. The camp had originally belonged to a Hungarian aristocratic family. I remember approaching it through thick lines of poplar trees on either side of the road.

Sometimes, two thousand young people would be there at once, and one could hear their singing and glorifying God everywhere. The sleeping quarters were one-half mile from the main camp, and in the mornings we often marched in groups, singing on our way there. Leaders watched and waited for us. Our unity and bonding, which only Christ can give, was beautiful to participate in and to behold. A positive experience like this builds and leads to feelings of acceptance, while a negative one only destroys the spirit.

But by 1950, the revival ran itself out. The Communist authorities called in the leaders and asked them what exactly was going on in the camp. When the leaders explained about the singing and other activities, that they were keeping the young people from alcohol, sex, and such, the authorities did not believe them. They could not imagine how this could be. They thought we were a political organization, and fearing a large group organizing a rebellion, they disbanded the group and took over the camp. They also broke up the Catholic Youth Organization. Then they outlawed any meeting whatsoever, requiring a permit which they, of course, would never grant.

What had happened during Lenin's time in Russia now continued under Stalin, engulfing all of Eastern Europe. Just as the Czarist regime was persecuted, along with the aristocracy and upper classes, so were the Hungarian upper middle class and the rich farmers, the "kulaks." The Communistic atrocities showed just how evil men can be in their ugly treatment of others.

My father and I were affected from the beginning. His belonging to the rich class, plus being influential in the old conservative regime, was a "red flag" to the Communists— and I don't mean their red flag. We were the stinking Bourgeois, the class enemy, and we had to be punished. They forced us to almost live like Gypsies, as I mentioned before, in our own home.

In 1951, the deportations began. The Communists brought young peasants from the countryside to educate them in the Communist cause. They were given the homes and apartments of the upper middle class families, who were then sent to live in the peasants' previous homes. At the railroad stations in the countryside, police watched the deportees from the cities, not allowing them to return. The people had no choice of where to live. Sometimes their "new homes" were shacks with mud floors and mice running everywhere.

For six weeks in Budapest, the bell would ring at six o'clock in the morning. If your name was on the black list, you had twenty-four hours to leave your home and go to your designated area. But my father was never on the list, though many of his friends were. I again considered it a miracle of God. He was protecting my father in the years he was approaching old age.

Even though we remained in Budapest, I could never get a white-collar job, in spite of my having a Doctorate in Law and Political Science by then. Yes, I had been able to go to the university during the years after the war. One time, I sought a job as a judge. The young Communist clerk looked at me and shook her head. "Not with your background," she said. So I worked for the railroad carrying tracks in ninety-degree heat or ten degrees below zero. Plus I worked in factories, and simply because I had had a privileged past life.

My good friend from my elementary school years, Al Fay, worked with me one time. He was carrying tar in a bucket when

149

he spilled some on his hand, badly burning himself. From his whole arm and fingers his skin was just hanging down. Often did I observe him checking his new skin as it left a mark. Then about twenty years later I heard that he died in a terrible accident. As he was chauffering some kids in a car, crossing railroad tracks, he had a heart attack in the middle—an oncoming train wiped them all out.

The university system in Hungary, Austria, and Germany were unique then. Positions in banks, the State Department, and other government areas required a Doctorate in Law. My father had one and so I had decided to get one, also. I was lucky to have started when I did, before the Communist clampdown. They would not have accepted me anywhere. But when the cannons fell silent in May of 1945, the government made it possible for veterans and others to finish one year of their education in just three summer months, which I did. Then I was able to continue.

All the professors in 1945 were Monarchists, or Royalists, talking about his Majesty the Emperor. But little by little, they were all thrown out and a new breed of professor replaced them. Republicans, they were called. Hungary was now a People's Republic when it had been a kingdom, although not the type of Republic that we think of in the United States.

By the time I received my degree in 1952, all the professors were hardcore Communists and I had studied Dialectical Marxism in every area—Economics, Statistics, Politics, and Labor Law. I had gone through three constitutional systems during my university years.

At the Doctorate level, all tests were oral. Our names were listed along with when and where to appear for our tests. Although the schedule may have said ten o'clock, the professors would sometimes not show up until three o'clock in the afternoon. But it wasn't necessarily their fault. Many of them were parliamentarians and had to attend morning sessions. So when they would finally get to the university, we students were already exhausted, having sat on "pins and needles" all day. Then the professors would lead us to their offices, which were richly furnished with sofas, desks, and chairs. Then the tests would begin.

Most professors taught from their own books. I had a professor in International Law who was the ambassador to the Vatican. For his test you could choose any material you wanted. He would usually listen to you for three or four minutes before taking over. My professor in cannon law was implicated with Cardinal József Mindszenty in Russian mock trials. In his memoirs, the Cardinal mentions how he was beaten and beaten for days. Amazing, as he was the Cardinal Bishop of Hungary, called the "Primate."

> Anyone who had not been interrogated in Andrassy Street cannot imagine the horrors that took place there. . .the major brought me back to the cell; "Remember this," he said, "the defendants here have to make confessions in the form that we want." A lieutenant entered. . .he came charging at me and kicked me with all his might. Both of us fell against the wall. The major produced a rubber truncheon, forced me to the floor, and began beating me.[21]

God gave me a great victory in the writing of my thesis, which was required before my Doctorate exam. It was customary, believe it or not, to buy notes of professors' lectures from a business for such purposes. The worst, though, was that a student could also hire someone to write the actual thesis. Because this was accepted, I saw nothing wrong with it. So I went ahead and paid for the whole thing. But I only read the first three pages of the thesis. When it came time for me to defend it, I had no idea how to answer the professor's questions. Needless to say, he did not accept my thesis.

When I wrote another thesis by myself for another professor, I passed with "flying colors." God taught me through this

---

21 Mindszenty, Cardinal József, *Memoirs* (New York: Mac-Millan, 1974).

experience that honesty is expected of a Christian. I learned to rely more on Christ, for He said, *"Apart from me, you can do nothing."* (John 15:5 NIV) He made me what I am today. He has become my strength, my truth, and my righteousness.

In 1951, before the completion of my education, my father became ill. I had never seen him sick at all. He had difficulty breathing, and had sleepless nights. I remember taking him to the hospital once or twice, and God started to reveal to me that I might lose a second parent. My father had already told his lawyer friend that he would probably die soon, but he never told me. I'm sure he didn't want to upset me.

After he was in the hospital a few days that last time, they transferred him to the intensive care unit. At six o'clock in the evening, on April 27, 1952, he died. I was with him and my last words he would hear were that God loved him. My father had told me once that when he was born, all the church bells were ringing. When he died, I heard the church bells ringing for vespers, as they always did in Hungary. With that, a whole era of my life was gone. I was on my own.

I went home to our cold house, where the heat would not be restored for four more years. We still used the iron stove that smoked for about an hour before spewing out any warmth. Then it took another hour to warm up the main room. In the bathroom, we used butane gas when we could get it. When I worked on the railroad, I would get up in the frigid mornings, wash with cold water, go out and work all day in sometimes well below freezing weather, and then come home to a cold house. The one that used to be filled with warmth, love, and hope.

Once my father died, I became the "president" of our house. Every state-confiscated house had to have a president, along with a committee. Our fruit trees were also nationalized, everyone in the house getting his or her own tree. Once, one of the lady residents brought me a plate of plums from her tree. I told her I couldn't accept them, but she pushed the plate towards me saying, "Why don't you accept it? Just take it—it is yours anyway."

But most of the time, life was gray, dreary, cold, and monotonous. We went to parades, out of "obligation," and watched the banners march by. They declared, "Stalin the Great is every-where and watching you." The Communists even changed his birthday to December 21, to divert people's attention away from Christmas. We always joked that December 21 was the darkest day of the year, which it is, of course, being the winter solstice.

Every business had a corner called a "red square," with Sta-lin's picture on the wall. At meetings there, if they saw you not clapping, you could lose your job. There was a countess whom they fired for that very reason. She broke down and started screaming. Once an elderly aristocrat I worked with, who now swept floors, told me he was lucky they let him do that work. He just hoped they would leave him alone, not hurt him, and let him live.

Another time, I worked in a factory that made sunglasses. The former owner was now the head manager. For a while I worked with a former nun from Notre Dame, a girl's high school in Europe. The Communist regime had done away with all religious groups by then, of course

Everyone had to work, but to change jobs was very difficult. I still have the red booklet that I had to carry in order to transfer to another position. It contains my history of where I worked, what I did, and my performance. If you took a sick day, you had to bring a written excuse from a doctor, and of course that was forever stamped in your book.

Each worker had to produce a certain amount. If the "norm" was not met, you could lose your job. Although I was consid-ered a good worker, a young manager stormed in once and told me to stop working. He explained to me that I had written down the "wrong" amount of work, not the "norm." I had to go the office where they said I might be handed over to the Secret Police. Yet I wasn't. Once again, God stepping in on my behalf. I was fired on the spot, however, never knowing why. Perhaps because I had been a member of the Bourgeois.

I had two architecture students living with me after my fa-ther died. Both had different attitudes about the oppression of the upper middle class. One never really saw or understood what I was going through, how much had been taken away from me. Thirty-three years later during my visit to Hungary, the other student said, "George, they persecuted you so much." More than forty years have passed since those days of suffering. Some may not believe that it happened—perhaps they don't want to deal with the reality. Even my children, along with their generation, have trouble imagining such dire circumstances.

Even if life was stark and hard in those days, I had Christ in my life and that changed my whole outlook. God somehow made me immune to the strife, because looking to Him brought me joy and security. Philippians 4:11 (NIV) says, *"For I have learned to be content whatever the circumstances."* I know that nothing can happen to me without God's knowledge, and therefore I am safe in His hands.

God's children, those who trust Christ as their personal Saviour, take solace in Hebrews 13:5 (NIV)—*"Never will I leave you; never will I forsake you."* We can be as happy as we will be in heaven. Our state of mind should not depend on our circumstances. For feelings can easily bury us in quicksand. In God we find contentment, when we rely on Him. He was there for me back then, just as He is here for me now.

Shake the Dust
Off Your Feet. . .
— a flight from tyranny

I brought two important things with me on my escape from Hungary, my baby book, and my father's cane made of Indian grapevine. He needed it for his arthritis, which I now have. But I accidentally left that gorgeous cane by a haystack, and would never see another one like it. Yet I had lost so much more than that, and not just in material goods. I imagine that an Austrian farmer has enjoyed that cane now for over forty years. . .

In the summer of 1956, there were signs that people wanted change, a way out of the terrible Soviet prison-life in Hungary. This attitude probably began when Nikita Krushchev, in a speech at the Communist Party's Twentieth Congress, denounced Stalin and his "cult of himself." The speech proved to be a turning point, and was meant to be a secret. Copies, however, were leaked across Eastern Europe. One even reached me in the countryside, where I was that summer.

Insurrection first surfaced openly at the Petofi Club, named after Hungary's greatest lyric poet in the nineteenth century. Ideas fostered demands, which seeped into the universities where revolutions often begin. Professors and students started to debate in the hallways, and soon the whole system was in an uproar. On October 23, 1956, the students filled the streets of Budapest, demonstrating before the parliament building.

Suddenly, the crowd pushed and shoved towards the radio station, demanding their right to broadcast their grievances. Then a tear gas bomb exploded in a young man's face, killing him. The revolution was no longer bloodless. Hungarian troops openly sided with the population, passing out rifles and ammunition. Waves of Russian tanks, which had already rolled across Hungary's border, rumbled into the streets of Budapest but quickly withdrew to the outskirts.

For ten days, until November 4, 1956, Hungary was a free nation. The people were united as one. It was beautiful to see, as the country had never been so free before, everyone feeling equal. It had always been close to a dictatorship, with three or four big landowners, including the Catholic Church. Forty percent of the land had been in the hands of just a few aristocratic families

There were hundreds of villages and cities ruled by one lord living in his big castle on a hill. Below him lived the tenants who were tied to the soil, just as in Russia. On Christmas, the peasant children received shoes and clothing, nothing more. There was even a law, the "law of the first night," allowing the lord to sleep with a tenant-bride before she consummated her marriage.

Unfortunately, Admiral Horthy, the Regent of Hungary, never carried out any soil reform. It then fell to the Russians and Communists to do as they saw fit. I myself never knew what true democracy was until coming to America.

But the peace of the revolution did not last. On November 4, 1956, in the early hours of the morning, we all woke to bombardments reminiscent of World War II. Russian tanks and troops reentered Budapest full force, without any difficulty, determined to capture the city. The battle raged right in the midst of a town of one million.[22] [23]

> Attention! . . . This is Imre Nagy speaking. . .
> President of the Council . . . of the Hungarian
> People's Republic. Today at daybreak Soviet

---

22 The following quotes are all from The Hungarian Revolution, edited by Melvin J. Lasky.

23 Lasky, Melvin J., editor, *The Hungarian Revolution, the Story of the October Uprising as Recorded in Documents, Dispatches, Eye-Witness Accounts, and World-wide Reactions* (New York: Frederick A. Praeger, Inc., Publishers, 1957).

forces started an attack against our capital . . . Our troops are fighting. The government is in its place.

—Free Radio Kossuth, 4 November

During the first twenty-four hours, Russian tanks and cannon fire crashed the principle resistance centres . . . but the young Hungarians [the Freedom Fighters] continued to fire on the Russians from the windows and housetops of their dwellings . . . the Russians answered each rifle shot with tank fire. The tanks, in a roar of thunder, bore down upon the houses from which shots were being fired, pointing their guns first at the ground floor, then at the first floor, the second, and the third. . .the houses were blown apart and crumbled; the inhabitants were either killed, or lay wounded on the ground . . .

—Michael Gordey France-Soir (Paris),
14 November

The arrangement was for the women to stand in doorways with machine guns. The men threw the Molotov cocktails into the tanks. If the cocktail did not go off, or if any Russian soldiers escaped, the women shot them down. We took most of our arms and ammunition from the Russians. One thing we were short of was bottles for the filling with petroleum to throw into the tanks.

—A student, age 27 Manchester Guardian,
21 November

We request every Western station which is able to receive our message, to transmit this in English, German, and French! We need help! The population of Budapest has no food! For lack of medicines and military help many persons are dying! We ask for food and arms! . . . Severe

fighting is going on in the 8th District of Budapest. The Russians have encircled the district and
the population is digging trenches and making
barricades. Russian army transports are arriving
at Budapest airfields [and] the East station [is]
crowded with Russians. Hungarian youth will
fight to their last breath. Hungary was always
the fortress of the West. The situation becomes
more difficult by the hour. Only military help
can save us. The whole nation pleads for help.

—Free Radio Roka, 5 November

At the moment, fighting is going on at the
capital . . . the railway bridge [is] entirely in
the hands of the Freedom Fighters. Some Russian tanks only dare to move in formations. In
many places, they have built barri cades along
the roads. Desperate fighting is going on. . .. [In
other parts of the country], the Russians hold the
barracks and have dug themselves in . . .

—Free Radio Rakoczi, 5 November

Please, forward our request to the Vienna Red
Cross! They should help! Several hospitals are in
flames! . . . Food and ammunition is becoming
scarce! Russians are launching extremely strong
attacks! When will the UN delegates arrive? . . .

—Free Radio Rakoczi, 5 November

. . . I saw small children standing by the tanks
and cursing the crews for what they had done.
"Do you really believe," one little girl was asking,
"that you have come to liberate us . . . ?" "You
unspeakable swine," another shouted. "You
won't get away with this!" It was the first time
the compulsory learning of Russian in Hungarian
schools had paid a dividend. The young Hungarians could tell the Russians what they thought of

them—and in their own language . . .

—Lajos Lederer
The Observer (London), 18 November

During the week of the revolution, I got involved in demonstrations. One cloudy day as I walked in a crowd, a woman passed by murmuring that such a cloudy, drizzly day occurred in November, 1918. She was no doubt referring to when Hungary lost World War I. It seemed our country was always on the losing side.

Yet God helped me stay alive. One of my father's best friend's nephew was shot and died instantly, simply walking by a window. I could have been killed just as easily while walking on the streets in those days, or standing in a crowd. I remember deciding to go to work one day and a machine gun went off, as if to say, "Stop working, there is a revolution on now."

In the end, five thousand youth were dead, and many others were shipped to Siberia. However, I believe it was the finest hour in the one-thousand years of Hungary's history. For once, the Hungarians were fighting against injustice, economic hardship, government brutality, and a forced class system. This was a revolution of the proletariat, the working class, and the intellectuals against a new system, one of foreign rule. They were striving to overthrow the establishment, not just revolt, but change things, seize the power of the state. Sadly, they did not achieve this goal.

Towards the end of November, I had thoughts that I could not stay in Hungary. What am I doing here in this land? I am persecuted. I don't have a future. I have no family here. I have an uncle in Vienna, and good friends of my parents in America. I asked God what to do. The Word of God, the circumstances, and the advice of believers all pointed toward my leaving my country.

I had a friend with whom I worked in a factory. A few years earlier, we had taken a winter trip through the Hungarian countryside. He was a photographer and we went from house to house, taking pictures and then sending them back from

Budapest. Although I enjoyed his company, my boots were always wet as we trudged through the snow, across fields and down dirt roads. I asked this friend if he would help me escape from Hungary. He said yes, that he would go with me. We agreed that on the morning of November 26, 1956, we would meet and leave together, to escape the miserable life we led in Budapest.

The night before we left, I took two very expensive paintings that had been my father's across the street to a surgeon's house. The frames were so big that I left them at home. One of the paintings was by an Austrian painter, Tina Blau. Even the Austrian imperial family owned some of her paintings. I never saw those paintings again. When I was to ask about them thirty years later on a trip to Budapest with my wife, I was told they had been sold.

While touring the Hungarian National Gallery on that same trip, the only time I would return to my homeland, I stopped before a familiar-looking painting, entitled "Sleeping Girl." I walked past it several times until I realized it had hung in my father's living room. One of my best friend's sons, a restorer in the gallery, took a picture of it and sent it to me. Today, I have a copy of the painting, in miniature, beautifully framed and hanging in my home.

Even if all of my father's paintings could be traced and proven to be part of my inheritance, Hungary would never let them out of the country. They are considered national treasures. Recently, it has been discovered that the Jewish treasures confiscated before and during World War II are difficult to trace and return to their rightful owners. Most of them were acquired legally and in good faith by the new owners, whether a museum, a gallery, or a private person. So they are not obligated to return them.

My father's paintings, our house, my life as I had known it, were all things that had not only been taken from me, but which I had now decided to leave behind, forever. My friend and I left my house very early on the date we had arranged. We walked down the hill, turned the corner, and I looked back one last time, at my parental home. I remember thinking how it had gone through a war, a siege, a revolution, and yet it still stood, against the backdrop of a city in shambles. I asked myself, "Will I ever see it again? Will it ever be rebuilt? Will I ever own it again?" Thirty years later when I returned, the bullet holes were still in its walls, a sorrowful reminder of the bombings, the shellings, the horror of those days.

Although I knew it was for the best and that God was calling me elsewhere, I felt a deep loss. A Christian is a patriot, so I was a Hungarian patriot, in spite of all that I had been through and how the present government treated me. Once I left, I would no longer have roots. I would not even be able to visit my paternal home where I had grown up. People have a hard time understanding what this is like. It is more than losing one's freedom. It is losing one's past, one's identity.

We did not really have a plan on how to escape. We did know that the streetcars were running, but we did not know how we could get to the border. Getting to the border zone would be difficult enough, but there were thirty miles between that and freedom. One could only enter this zone with government permission, which we were not about to get.

My last recollections of Budapest before returning many years later, were the Russian tanks guarding the bridgeheads as we crossed them going to the railroad station. People were milling around everywhere, and we discovered that only one rail line was open in the direction of the border. We could hardly believe it. A flood of refugees started leaving the country as soon as the Russians reoccupied the capital on November 4, 1956. Altogether, by January, 1957, some 170,000 would leave. Yet we were able to buy tickets that very day and board the train.

We met a young woman on the train and she joined us. She wanted to reach her grandmother in Uruguay. Our plan was to go to Hegyeshalom, the main border station between Austria and Hungary, and from there we did not know. As the train neared the station, I noticed that the other passengers either lowered their voices to whispers, or got off, to find their own way across to the border.

The conductor approached us and, leaning forward, quietly

told us that we should not go as far as the border station of Austria and Hungary. The Hungarian Secret Police was watching it very closely that day. So we detrained at the next stop, and started walking. We did not know where we were, or how we would approach the border zone.

So I had to rely on God, step by step, as Abraham and Moses did throughout their journeys.[24] Many times on the way, we would be able to see only one step ahead, and that left us not just weary but feeling vulnerable. But the more I trusted God, the less I feared our situation, and the more faith I had to continue our journey.

We started out on what appeared to be a highway. We saw a truck coming with people hanging off of it, so we decided to join them. Nobody said a word and the weather was drizzly, cold, and wet. The trailer stopped at a farmhouse. We were told that at dark, a guide would lead us across the border zone.

Darkness comes soon at the end of November. Our guide, a stocky young man, arrived and instructed us on how we should behave: when he ducked, we ducked; when he ran, we ran; and no talking All this was not easy in groups of four or five, some people with babies. I carried a little one myself for a while.

The border had been open for twelve days when the Freedom Fighters were in control,' but after that, the situation had changed. When my group of refugees crossed the border, we had to go through both Hungarian and Russian lines. Our guide explained that the Russians shoot up flares. When one flare goes up to the right, we would pull to the left. When it goes left, we would go right. It happened exactly as he said it would. Then he stopped, telling us that the border was only two hundred yards away. "There is a road ahead," he said. "When you cross it, you will more or less be in Austrian territory."

But crossing it, we were inundated by a powerful flashlight and a voice shouting "Halt! Stop!" We were caught, just a few yards from our freedom. We were herded to some military barracks where we sat on bunks, tired and wet. The Hungarian border guards told us they would hand us over to the Russians,

---

24 Refer to the books of Genesis and Exodus.

who would then take us back to Budapest. We knew that meant an automatic five-year prison sentence, with no parole.

A truck arrived, not a Russian truck but a Hungarian one. The others with us wanted to get on it, but they were told to stay back. Only my friend, the girl who had joined us, and I were allowed to climb up. We knew for sure, as we drove through a Russian patrol and were told to duck, that we were not en route to Budapest. We had to stop and the Russians stood outside and searched the truck, but not thoroughly enough to find us. Within a few minutes, the truck stopped again and the three of us got off.

The lights in the distance were in Austria, we were told. If we didn't keep going towards those lights, we could go in circles and not even know it. A few steps into Austria, we heard a machine gun. Whether or not it was shooting at us, we would never know. We kept going and going on that damp, gloomy November night. It must have been around two o'clock in the morning when we saw car and jeep lights in the distance. Austrians were searching for and finding Hungarian refugees. Once some headlights passed in front of us, but we weren't close enough for anyone to see us.

The girl with us grew very tired and wanted to sit down. We found a haystack that kept us somewhat dry. After a few minutes, we heard voices in the distance, but didn't know if they were Austrian or Hungarian. But it did not take me long to make them out to be Austrian, as they spoke German, the language I had learned from my mother. We stood up so they would see us, and they welcomed us as if we were long lost friends.

After a while, as the darkness receded and it became light, we reached an Austrian village. There in a small store, I immediately noticed things I had not seen for fifteen years—oranges and bananas. I was beginning to sense freedom.

A Land of Milk and Honey. . .

— a wondrous new life

I began to taste the American way of life. A big man asked me if I wanted a Coke. I had heard of Coca-Cola®, but not "Coke." I remember listening to music on a bus's speaker system playing "Volari," an Italian song from the early 50's. It reminded me of Europe, but I would come to love American composers and entertainers more. To me, they are the best in the world. . .

Before I left Hungary, a good friend and classmate said to me, "George, you are now going to a free country, but don't forget your real freedom is in the Lord." Those words have always stayed with me. It was a great feeling to be free in Austria, and later in America, but spiritual freedom, only found in Christ, is the most important kind in anybody's life. Without freedom in Christ, one is a prisoner and restless.

We are actually all prisoners of ourselves, of our nature, with its selfishness, antagonism, corruption, and superstition. Some people say that all men are basically good. This is not so. *"We all have sinned and fall short of the glory of God,"* says the Apostle Paul in Romans 3:23 (NIV). Christ says in John 8:36 (NIV), *"So if the Son sets you free, you will be free indeed."* He knew we were prisoners of our sins.

But there is only one escape, in Christ: *"Whoever hears my word and believes in Him who sent me has eternal life."* (John 5:24 NIV) Eternal life starts exactly when a person believes and trusts in Christ. Not in the future, not after death, but in the change that takes place at that moment. There is release from one's old nature, replaced by God's new nature and His grace.

I remember my first thoughts in that small Austrian village were a mixture of "thank God we made it; we were not harmed; we are young and have a life before us." But all of these thoughts would not really sink in for quite a while. In those first morning's hours, I recognized some people whom had been caught by the Hungarian patrol the same time we had. They must have just run after the truck and jumped on it.

Later, busses took us toward Vienna, and on the way we passed by the Esterhazy Palace, dominating the town of Eisenstadt in the Province of Burgenland. Haydn composed some of his works there, serving as its musical director for thirty years, from 1761 to 1796. The castle was built between 1663 and 1672 by the great Hungarian noble family whose name it bears, and who had holdings not just in Hungary and Austria, but all over Europe.

The Esterhazy family, who still owns the castle, is one of the oldest and most prominent families among Hungarian aristocracy, tracing their roots back to Attila the Hun in the thirteenth century. All the family members were strong Hungarian Nationalists, supportive of Habsburg rule, actually enjoying a larger fortune than the emperors did. They were patrons of the arts, music and science.

We ended up in military barracks that probably still housed soldiers from the Austro-Hungarian monarchy. There, I found a phone and called my uncle in Vienna. When I arrived at his and his wife's apartment, he told me, "I knew you would come." I had written him a card from Budapest during the revolution, but had never expected him to receive it.

I did not really know my uncle. I had probably seen him last when I was a little boy, visiting with my mother, but I did not even remember that. He was a very intelligent gentleman and spoke several languages. He considered anyone who didn't know about opera to be totally uneducated. Yet he was kind and thoughtful. I will always be thankful to him that he opened his home to me.

Vienna in November and December of 1956, was full of Hungarian refugees. I heard more Hungarian spoken on the streets than German, and I met people whom I had not seen in Budapest for twenty years. I ran into many Christian friends whom I knew from the Hungarian national revival. We would meet off and on in one of Vienna's Lutheran churches. However, the meetings were somewhat depressing after all we had gone through, not knowing what the future would bring. Yet we prayed and talked.

The American embassy was a huge building, besieged by thousands of people all day and every day. American troops were still in full force in Austria, it being the only country that Russia had occupied and had to leave. In 1954, a separate peace treaty to this effect had been signed in the Belvedere Palace in Vienna. The Austrians gave them flowers as they left, not out of gratitude or love, but out of joy to be rid of them. Wherever they had been, they left behind unbelievable destruction, of streets, buildings, and the government.

On one of my first days in Vienna, I wrote to my parents' best friends, the Danos, now in America. My father helped save their bank during the depression, and my father arranged for them to stay in a hospital. Many rich Jewish people hid in hospitals during the Nazi persecution, or converted to other religions if that would save them. The Danos replied with a telegram that they were expecting me with "open arms."

Christmas and New Year's rolled around, and although my uncle and his wife were invited to quite a few parties and celebrations, I did not want to go along. I was still overwhelmed by the turmoil of the Hungarian Revolution. When five thousand young people had just given their lives for a great and worthy cause, I did not want to be "merrymaking."

I remember walking on the street one night with my uncle's wife, always looking back. She asked me why, and I told her that people behind me made me nervous. Every noise sounded like a machine gun to me. I still suffer from those postwar symptoms today, although they have lessened over the years.

Planes had been taking groups to different countries, and the day soon came for me to say good-bye to my uncle and his wife. I flew to Salzburg, called the Mozart city because he was born there. He was considered the child prodigy of Austria, composing at the age of twelve and playing before Empress Maria Theresa.

Along with other refugees, I went to a camp near Salzburg for instructions on the American way of life. For example, in Europe you talk about the next street, but in America, the next block. They taught us how to convert temperatures from Celsius to Fahrenheit. Today, I still convert from Fahrenheit to Celsius to tell what the weather is or will be like.

Salzburg is in the most western part of Austria, in the middle of the Alps. Germany is only a few miles away, and Munich is not much farther. I remember walking one afternoon in the forest and out of nowhere appeared a border guard, telling me to turn around because I was approaching the border.

Now, when I see news about refugee camps, I know what the inhabitants are going through. The camps have their own reality, not just different from the life the refugees have left behind, but different from the outside world. Everything you own is above your bed on a shelf. And you not only sleep on your bed, but you live on your bed, making yourself as comfortable as you can. It is the center of your world.

I became anxious to get on with it, to go to the United States. It was nice to walk in the forests, and I enjoyed staying in such a cultural city, but I was ready to start my new life. But when you are anxious about something, you try to hurry it along. This has always been a part of my childish side. I want to have everything now, in the present, right away, and not later. I have even made demands of God to move things along a bit faster.

Yet a believer must always count God in his plans. When we pray, we must add "if God wills it." In the Garden of Eden, there was only one will—God's. As soon as Adam and Eve sinned, there was also a human will, and the two wills would constantly clash forever. When one is converted to Christ, however, the desire for God's will is restored. Taking back your own will, then, can cause trouble.

So learning to trust God and accept His will often entails waiting—waiting for an answer, waiting for things to get better, and in my case in 1957, waiting to start my future. I had learned a lesson in patience when the day finally arrived, after I had been in the camp for two weeks, that my name was on the list to fly to America.

We flew across Europe to Dublin, Ireland. There we were invited for supper by the airport authorities. Then we flew that same night across the Atlantic to the United States, a total of about nine thousand miles.

At dawn, our stewardess told us we were flying over New York. The plane landed in New Jersey at Camp Kilmer, which had been a World War II training camp. United States troops had been shipped to Europe from there. I stepped from the plane and looked around. The sky was blue with a few clouds driven by the wind. On that day, March 2, 1957, I had no one and nothing.

I stayed at that camp for ten days. All of the refugees were to be sent to different parts of the country, where church groups and sponsors were waiting for them. Mr. Danos, my sponsor, arrived at the camp carrying a bouquet of flowers, the Hungarian way of welcoming friends. We traveled to Wichita, Kansas. Any European coming to America is gripped by the immensity of this country. I certainly was on that first train ride, as it lasted three days and three nights.

When I arrived in Wichita, a delegation from the First Presbyterian Church was waiting for me. I saw myself on television that same evening. The next day, Mr. Schaeffer came from the Counsel of Churches to help me with anything "official." He gave me the choice to stay with another Hungarian man or with an American family I chose a fine American couple, the Amstutz. He was a geologist and they had three children. Later, he became Vice President of the Fourth National Bank.

Within a week, I had my first job, folding envelopes at a printing press. I earned one dollar an hour. I found that English was not too hard for me to learn, as it shares the Germanic root of the German language. I was off to a good start.

That Fall, I met my future wife, Jane. She belonged to the same First Presbyterian Youth Group that I did. I noticed that she seemed more spiritual and intelligent than the others. She taught English composition at East High School, one of the best schools in the nation at that time. She likes to tell people the amusing story that I did not accept a date with her until I finished the banking course I was taking at the time.

Through her prodding, I went to Wichita University to earn a teaching certificate. This was not as easy as it sounds. To start all over in a foreign country is difficult, especially when one is not that young anymore. Although I was thirty-one years old when I came over, I tried to act as if I was American, when in reality, I was very much Hungarian. I had to work my way up, step by step, in school, in language, and in culture.

I brought my "evangelistic spirit" with me wherever I went. I joined the Inter-varsity Christian Fellowship at school. We organized Bible studies, and talked about the Lord to students. My first week in this country, I was invited to Friends University, a Quaker college. I spoke there before the student body. Going on and on, I couldn't finish until I was pulled back to my seat. At least I was witnessing for the Lord.

When we were dating, Jane invited me to meet her parents in her hometown of Marshall, Missouri, eighty miles east of Kansas City. I took the bus. Jane's mother was an English teacher at the college level. Her father was a prosecuting district attorney, and he and his brother practically ran the town.

While there, Jane and I walked in the park, swam in the park's swimming pool, and enjoyed a real American summer, hot but carefree. As we drove home, we stopped and then I asked her if she would marry me, but I added, only if she would serve the Lord with me. Since the Lord Jesus Christ is the center of my life, I cannot leave Him out of anything, especially not marriage.

I lived as a single man in different places. I was lonely and everything was new and strange. It was more of a cultural shock than anything else, from the conservative "old world" to the progressive "new world." At one time, I shared an apartment with a fine Christian boy, Marvin Schrag. His parents were farmers. Years later, after we were both married, we wrote to each other but eventually lost touch.

My first teaching job was during the school year of 1960 to

1961, in Biola, Kansas, thirty miles from Wichita. Mr. Loewenguth, the Superintendent of Schools for the county and a fine gentleman, got me that job. It turned out that his wife and my future mother-in-law grew up together and were good friends. I was driven out to Biola by an older teacher and often had to be back there in the evening for a basketball game. The schoolhouse was in the middle of a field and grades one through twelve were all under one roof.

As the school year ended, the Principal asked me to take the senior graduating class to Galveston, Texas. He came along with his wife. What a great time we all had. I was engaged to a fine Christian girl and my life was before me, in a new country, with unlimited possibilities. I was healthy and the Lord encompassed me in His arms.

Jane and I married in 1961, and spent our honeymoon in a cabin in Green Mountain Falls, Colorado, near Colorado Springs. It belonged to the Cooper family, who had helped me get established when I first arrived as a Hungarian refugee, four years before. Mr. Cooper was a very prominent lawyer in Wichita. I still keep in touch with some of his children.

Our son, Paul, was born the first year of our marriage, an incredible experience for me. I could have been killed so many times, and yet there I was, with a son. Our first home was near the city park. As we were both teaching, we hired a nanny for Paul. She always waved good-bye to us from the window, with Paul in her arms.

Then I went back to school for a Masters Degree in German at the university in Lawrence, Kansas. Jane's whole family had gone there, her father, her mother, her uncle, and her sister. I spent a cold, windy winter there without my wife and baby son, but the campus was beautiful when all the trees bloomed in the spring.

It was then that Ms. Schoonover, the Personnel Director from Littleton, Colorado, came to interview prospective teachers. He hired me to teach German for their new school, Arapahoe High School, that they were building. We arrived in Littleton on July 1, 1963. All around us was countryside. Much has changed since then.

Our son Paul was one year old and I remember the day he started walking. Our daughter, Grace, was born two years later. At first, she was completely bald, when girls are usually born with much hair.

I taught German and History at the high school. For twenty years, Jane would have a Good News Club in the basement of our home. Children between the ages of six and twelve came every Friday to hear about Jesus. Many found the Lord Jesus as their personal Saviour. A neighbor boy, who came quite regularly, became an aeronautical engineer. When he met his future wife, who worked with Campus Crusade for Christ, the Lord led him to leave his high-paying job to join her in her work. Later, he came to visit my wife to thank her for being instrumental in his Christian life.

I started a street ministry about the same time Jane started her Good News Club. Then, more than ten years ago, I became involved in the prison ministry of the Salvation Army. I have led Bible studies in prisons around the Denver metro area. Many men have accepted Jesus as their personal Saviour, and continue to come to the Bible studies. I have received letters from former inmates, saying that their "meeting" the Lord changed their lives.

But our life was not all "work and no play." My wife trained two golden retrievers and we took the children to dog shows, and to their swimming competitions. Our children were both all-American swimmers, and my son earned his way through a private college with a swimming scholarship.

After that, he received his Masters Degree in California. A handsome six-foot man, he works for a cellular phone company where he handles the international accounts. He has a big home in Laguna Beach. At this writing, he is getting married in Hawaii in only a few days. Our daughter Grace also graduated from a Colorado university and now runs her own pet-sitting business in California. Her husband is in computers. She was always her father's girl, both beautiful and thoughtful. Recently, she came for ten days to help us when I had knee-replacement surgery.

These two children were our greatest gift from God and formed our happy family. Jane and I raised them to follow the path that we have, living for the glory of God. At our daughter's wedding, I contemplated all of the amazing miracles it took for me to even be there. I spoke about the blessings of the Lord.

Indeed, even in times of war, loss, and persecution, He has a reason behind everything we go through. Sometimes it is to bring us to Him. Other times it is a lesson we must learn, such as trusting Him in all circumstances. With me, it was both of these things, so I would be able to serve Him for the rest of my life. With a believer, it cannot be otherwise.

For "those who bear the mark of pain are never really free, for they owe a debt to the ones who still suffer,"[25] as well as to God. He saved me from not only political tyranny, but most important from the bondage of sin. He gave me a new life. My duty has been and still is to thank Him by sharing His love and forgiveness with others—through my words, through my actions, and now through this book. . .

---

25 Albert Schweitzer

Epilogue

Here we are, two years from the twenty-first century. For thirty years, our lives went smoothly. Nothing went wrong. We were a happy, busy family. Sometimes, I wondered how long those problem-free years would last. Then tragedy struck. . .

We had been married for thirty-one years when Jane had her first stroke. We were on our way to our jail ministry when suddenly, she could not talk. In the hospital, the doctors told us that the tendency to have strokes is inherited. Many in her family, her parents, her grandparents, an uncle, and an aunt, had all suffered from strokes. We visited her family many times after her father had his first stroke. I would help him walk. Then he was in a wheelchair and I never saw him out of it again.

They kept my wife in the hospital, and as I drove home in the early Fall darkness, desperation and loneliness overwhelmed me. I felt my life would change drastically. Jane and I had been able to travel, which we both loved, since our retirement. Now, that might not be possible. I got ready for bed and knelt down. I did not understand how this could happen, and I cried out to the Lord, my soul weeping.

For a few days, Jane stayed in that chasm between life and death. Our children came home for about three days, but they both had to get back to their jobs. Then Jane began to recover. She went through therapy everyday. What a sad picture, I thought, as I watched my wife, a former teacher, such an intelligent woman, being taught how to read, write, and speak.

Everyday I would go home to an empty house and listen to the rain. I felt joyless and burdened, as if I had lost all the freedom I had gained escaping Hungary. But I knew that if I would have to, I could take care of Jane the rest of our lives.

The doctors transferred Jane to a glorified nursing home for more therapy, where she spent endless hours waiting to be taken to the dining room to eat. I compared her situation to a concentration camp, where people live for lunch and supper, nothing in between but hours and hours of grueling work in unbearable heat or cruel cold. Of course, this wasn't the exact same experience, but waiting sometimes can be as awful as hard work, if not worse. Plus the air in the nursing home was stale.

When I would wheel my wife down to the dining room, we would pass the same man and he'd ask us if we had room to get by, otherwise he would stare, nothing more. One lady liked to sit beside Jane because she thought her a lady. She was right— my wife is a fine lady. I am glad she is still with me. I thank the Lord each and every night when I hear her breathing beside me in bed.

But while she was in the nursing home, I got more and more depressed, and that scared me. I knew that a child of God should not be depressed because he should always look to God for his victory. I practiced giving things over to God for years and it really worked. But this latest experience seemed more difficult than anything else I had gone through, even the war. My depression hung on.

When Jane first came home, I was left to do everything for her and around the house—the shopping, the cooking, the housework, the yard, and the finances became my responsibility. Of course, they had been the whole time since she was sick. But this was more difficult, because I also had to take care of her, and needed to maintain the semblance of a normal, comfortable home, for her sake as well as mine.

Soon, Jane started to read and write well enough to want to take up driving lessons, so she could drive again and, in that way, regain some of her freedom. Then one day I noticed a relapse in her speech. She had had another stroke. This one ravished more of her functions than the first one.

Now, she can no longer read or write. Neither can she point out the date on a calendar. Her mind is excellent, but her ability to communicate has simply vanished. Besides all this, she has chronic blood clots, with one foot swollen two times the normal size. Plus the arthritis in her back gives her constant pain, so much so that she can hardly walk anymore.

After her second stroke, we became more and more homebound, and friends, it seemed, slowly fell away. Some people mean well, but they neither know what to do or what to say. They just don't know what it is like to be so sick, or to care for such a sick person. Others, like Job's three friends, lash out with their tongues, giving worn-out advice as if they know what our life is like.

Some come to visit and invite us out. They organize ladies to stay with Jane while I go to my jail ministries, knowing that the Bible study I lead is a tremendous blessing to me as much as the prisoners.

I call it my lifeline—my way to not just get away but to be connected to the outside world, doing something for the Lord again, although I know taking care of Jane is a ministry unto itself. For example, many former inmates have written to me, expressing their appreciation. This work is invaluable to me, boosting my spiritual life in this most difficult time. As in Budapest when God uplifted me, He comforts me now, expressing His love for me.

Jane does not sleep well at night, and I need to cover her up many times over. During these "half-sleepless" nights, I find solace only in my narrow hallway of dreams. As the main caregiver, I find myself tired, rundown, but I have to remain strong and healthy. So I go to the recreation center to exercise, and I also have free time when a nurse takes Jane to "aquacize." I have also joined a caregivers group where we share our thoughts and emotions. For these small breaks, I am grateful. Jane also has a ladies Bible study that meets at our house once a week.

Yet the days remain endless, extending into evenings and nights full of stillness, when my loneliness hits. We are struggling, my wife and I. Two shut-ins together, who can't always avoid friction. I saw the same situation during the war when people were in close quarters, day after day, with no real life, and the life they once had gone forever. And these people had not even known each other before, much less cared for each other the way Jane and I still do.

I do not understand God's reasons behind Jane's impairment, for we had been so active for Him in the past. Sometimes I can hardly believe this has happened. I feel sorry for myself, barely able to remember our healthy years. I read in a book review that a quadriplegic saw a lighthouse from his hospital bed and called it his hope. But my lighthouse, my hope, is Christ. He said, *"I am the light."* (John 8:12 NIV) The psalmist says *"The Lord is my light."* (Ps. 27:1 NIV)

Yet Christ is not just my light—He is my salvation. I fall, but with His strength, I get up. I can be down, but He lifts me up. I can feel hopeless, but Christ helps me trust in Him. As the psalmist said, *"For You have been my hope."* (Ps. 71:5 NIV)

Hope and faith go together. We can look to God with confidence in His loving care, even if circumstances logically counter that conviction. Abraham's faith kept his hope in God when human discernment had long before declared things impossible. Moses followed God when the journey looked bleak. With God, everything is possible. I know, for I lived through a horrible war and am a better person for it.

I am living another war now, battling myself as much as my situation. I no longer see God's plan for my life. All at once, all I knew had changed. So I ask God, "What's next?" I often pray as I read the Bible. *"Why have you forgotten me?"* Psalms 42:9 NIV asks. *"Why have you forgotten me?"* I pray, *"Father, this is my hope and faith in you, that you will show me again your ways and your mercy, that you have not forgotten me."*

Recently, the Lord gave me a verse that keeps coming back to me: *"For I know the plans I have for you, declares the Lord. Plans to prosper you and not to harm you, plans to give you hope and a future."* (Jer. 29:11 NIV) God's plan, however, is our coming to Him through the blood of His Son, Jesus Christ. We cannot connect with God without that. We cannot know of His blessings. And we certainly cannot have the kind of blind faith it takes to trust Him.

As God led me in the past, long ago in my homeland of Hungary, He still leads me today. Just as I did not know where my steps were taking me, as I walked through the rain that cold

November night I escaped into Austria, I am completely dependent on Him to lead me the way now.

For this, I glorify Him, even if my gratitude and praise do not come easy. He is the center of my heart and my life. Without Him, I would be nothing. Ah, but with Him, I have everything, even when my world seems to be falling apart.

George's children in front of Neuvirth Villa in 2005